The Back Nine:
How to Play Your Best Golf EVER in Later Life

BY
Dr. Skip Everitt

Foreword by Tom Jenkins

Library of Congress Control Number: 2012903101
CreateSpace
North Charleston, SC

ISBN: 1456372173
ISBN-13: 978-145637217

TABLE OF CONTENTS

DEDICATION

To Lynda, my partner in golf and in life for over forty-five years and the official "first reader" for this book.

To Randy and Beth Davis, my brother-in-law and sister-in-law who, with Lynda and I, make up the foursome of a lifetime.

The love and unfailing support of these three people are truly priceless.

Left to Right- Beth Davis, Randy Davis, Lynda Everitt, Skip Everitt

The Eighteen Chapters: A Roadmap to Rebuilding a Golf Game

The following chapters provide details about how to play your best golf in your later years. The lessons and principles—eighteen of them—are both memories of my own experience and ideas gleaned from interviews with players, coaches, and teachers who have helped thousands of avid senior golfers to maintain a competent and satisfying level of play.

In the spirit of reality shows and programs, I decided to reinvent myself with the help of several professional teachers, coaches, and therapists. Could a once-elite-level golfer with a former handicap of 5 and a current handicap of 14 regain his former status as a competent player?

The answer is YES, because I was willing to embrace the lessons of this blueprint for recovery. I did it. So can you.

Golf is the game of a lifetime. Neither my life nor my golf game is over. This book can restore your game and revitalize your life.

FOREWORD:
A Golf Champion's
Perspective

By Tom Jenkins, winner of eight tournaments on the PGA and Champions Tour, ranked ninth on the Champions Tour all-time money-winning list.

Why I Started Playing Golf

My first love in sports was baseball. After a very successful Little League career, at the age of twelve, I tore a muscle fiber in my pitching arm. My baseball career was over. My father and older brother were playing golf at the time, and I decided to follow them around and learn the game. At the age of fifteen, I woke up one day addicted to the game of golf.

How I Made the Decision to Join the Senior (Champions) Tour

After ending my regular tour career in 1985, I started my own short-game school in 1991. I didn't really think about the senior tour until a few years later. I didn't play much competitive golf during my teaching days, but because I had to demonstrate what I was teaching, my short game stayed very sharp. In the summer of 1997, I filed my entry for the Champions Tour Q School. I crammed a year's worth of practice into a few months and managed to finish tenth. Thanks to teaching the short school all those years, I hadn't lost my touch and feel around the greens. This finish gave me conditional membership for the upcoming tour season. It had been thirteen years since I had competed on the regular tour, so my future on the Champions Tour was unknown. Despite this long absence from tour golf, the decision to join the Champions Tour was easy. I wasn't making much money teaching, and the thought of having another opportunity to do something I loved jumped out at me. As they say, "When opportunity knocks..." I'm glad I opened the door!

How I Prepared for the Champions Tour Q School

First, my main focus was fitness. I began working out with a personal trainer. The results of working out led to my new belief that fitness is 90 percent of the game.

I began developing a positive attitude that I could really do this again and be a champion.

I also changed my grip from the standard Vardon (overlapping) grip to an interlocking grip. With practice, this eventually led to playing golf from left to right, instead of frequently hooking my shots and being afraid of the left side of the golf course.

My Advice for Senior Golfers That Will Have the Most Immediate Impact on Your Game

Start or get back to working out. Flexibility and core strength are the keys.

The second activity is to practice more around the greens. At a senior age, there isn't enough time to make major changes in swing habits. The game is all about scoring, so learn a better short game.

And Then There Are Slumps

Slumps happen to everyone. The never-give-up attitude certainly applies here. When having a slump during a round, there is a fine line between shooting 72 or 82. One must learn to stay focused on the main objective, which is scoring. Even on days when the rhythm and timing are not there, you must learn to keep the ball in play and get the ball into scoring positions. Giving up is NEVER an option!

Becoming a Winner

Being prepared mentally and physically will produce a winning outcome. Controlling one's thoughts, visualizing positive results, staying in the moment, executing one shot at a time, and expecting to be a contender all contribute to building success. CONFIDENCE is what all winners have over someone who never wins.

Plan Your Next Season and Set Goals
I give myself a couple of months prior to the coming season to get physically ready.

I begin my short work about a month and a half before the first event.

My full-swing work begins a month prior to the season.

My main enduring goal is to make sure I'm ready to have some fun playing golf. Having a second chance at this age to work at something one loves to do should be cherished. Having fun is the key.

My playing goals are to win and to finish in the top thirty players each year. After my first year, I knew that I could still compete with the best. I began expecting to be at the top of the list each and every year.

Also, beginning a new season is all about creating the enthusiasm again to get back to the competition.

My Philosophy about Practice
I feel that the golf swing is all about timing and rhythm. At my age (sixty-plus), I don't hit as many balls as in the past. When I practice, all I'm looking for is correct timing and rhythm. Sometimes it takes fifteen minutes, and sometimes it takes forty-five

minutes. Once I feel that timing and rhythm are in place, I stop.

Let the Magic Happen

I personally benefitted from the books written by winning coaches. From them I learned that the adrenaline rush of competition must be cherished—and controlled. Feeling nervous and uncertain are signs of negativity and will block out the positive effects of an attitude of "Let the magic happen!" Every time I have a crucial shot or putt, I consider it a possible magic moment.

Final Thoughts and Praise for This Book

This book, *The Back Nine: How to Play Your Best Golf EVER in Later Life*, is a guidebook for you to make the magic happen.

Read it for the rest of your life as a golfer. I believe that this book will increase your satisfaction about your golf game and add more fun to all aspects of your life.

Skip Everitt has put together over 150 time-tested and stimulating strategies for our lives as seniors.

ABOUT THE BOOK

A Note about the Title

This is not a book that promises you will hit the ball as far as you did in your twenties, thirties, or forties. It does not claim that you will win your club championship or qualify for the U.S. Amateur. What it does claim is that if you commit to personal fitness, proper practice, the right equipment, an attitude of hope, and the development of the mindset of a winner, you can play the best golf possible at this stage of life.

Realistically, you may have to move up to the next tee box, work particularly hard on your short game, and develop a reasonable plan for playing and sustaining a better golf game. You will be able to say, "That was a great drive for ME," or "That round of golf was fun and satisfying for ME."

About twelve years ago, I played a round on the Saujana Golf and Country Club course in Kuala Lumpur, Malaysia. I hired a class-A caddy to help me with the rolling terrain and undulating greens. A week before, he had caddied for Ernie Els, the winner of the Malaysia Open.

At the time, I was a 6 handicap and was on my way to scoring in the mid-70s for that day's round. I was, frankly, full of myself. On a relatively short par 5, I wanted to go for the green in two. I turned to my caddy and said, "What would Ernie Els hit from here?" He replied without hesitation, "You are not Ernie Els—lay up with an eight iron."

Skip Everitt and Ernie Els' caddie in Malaysia

I am not Ernie Els or Tom Jenkins. However, I am a happy, healthy, and competitive golfer who is playing the game I love, and I am experiencing those exquisite moments when I hit a shot that is as good as anyone has ever hit that shot. These moments and these days of playing beautiful courses with true ladies and gentlemen are priceless.

A Note on Gender

The Back Nine: How to Play Your Best Golf EVER in Later Life is written for both men and women. Whenever possible, I use "he or she" or "his or her" to describe an example. However, many times I will use the male gender since the golfer in the incident from which the example is taken was a man (or men).

There are no references in the book to the differences in men and women's golf.

I encourage you to go to **www.backninebook.com** and initiate or contribute to the blog about differences in the golf games of men and women. I believe that it will be an interesting and helpful discussion.

Meet the Experts

The following people agreed to serve as my expert panel. Without them this book would have limited credibility. Their experiences in golf, health, fitness, nutrition, and aging make this book a powerful roadmap for playing your best golf EVER in later life.

TOM JENKINS

Tom was born in Houston, Texas, and played collegiate golf for the University of Houston, where he was a member of the 1970 NCAA Division I National Championship golf team. In 1975, he won the regular tour's IVB-Philadelphia Golf Classic in a Monday playoff against Johnny Miller. Prior to joining the Champions Tour in 1997, Tom served as lead instructor for the Dave Pelz Short Game School. Tom won his first Champions Tour event in 1999 and has added six more victories as a member of the senior circuit. At the end of the 2011 season he was ninth on the all-time money-winnings list for the Champions Tour.

SHANNON FOLEY

Shannon is the owner and an instructor at Encore Pilates in Gainesville, Florida. She is a former dancer, volleyball player, and runner. She is Gold Certified through the Pilates Method Alliance and Stott Pilates. She is also a rehabilitation instructor and trainer. In addition, Shannon is a physical therapist who has worked with the highly regarded Houston Ballet, the University of Florida's outpatient physical therapy at Shands Hospital, and the University of Florida's student healthcare center. Shannon was interviewed for Chapter Six of this book.

JOHN REGER

John is founder and president of Briefcase Golf, a marketing, media, and events-planning company in Gainesville, Florida.

He is a twenty-nine-year member of the PGA and has served in various roles as an officer of the North Florida PGA Board. John has served as a starter/announcer for the Outback Champions Tour event in Tampa since 1989. He currently produces and hosts *Briefcase Golf,* a syndicated radio show heard across the state of Florida. John is a founding board member and equity partner of Razor Golf Inc. He has served as the general manager, director of golf, and head golf professional at four Florida country clubs.

PREFACE

From the Football Field to the First Tee

*"They say that golf is like life, but don't believe it.
Golf is more complicated than that."*
—Gardner Dickinson, PGA professional and cofounder of the
Champions Tour

As I tried to breathe, all I could hear was Coach yelling, "Get up and run it out, Everitt!" I was fifteen years old and a third-string quarterback for East Atlanta High School. I had played football since the fifth grade, with some success as a running back and linebacker. However, I had developed two problems since those relative glory days on the gridiron:

1. I had not grown much since the seventh grade. Being 5' 7" and 130 pounds worked well at twelve years old, when only a few guys were substantially heavier and taller than I. But at fifteen I was 5' 8'' and up to 136. Now the same guys who had been only a little bigger than I three years before were six feet tall and 180 pounds.

2. In the summer between the eighth and ninth grade, I noticed that I could not read fine print or see the names on some of the street signs in my

neighborhood. After a visit to the ophthalmologist, I was deemed "near-sighted with astigmatism." From that day on, I wore glasses until 1964, when I broke my glasses making a header in a college soccer game. That is when my parents decided it was time for me to try contact lenses.

But back to high school football. Back to lying on my back like an overturned turtle. Back to trying to breathe and feeling a sharp pain in my left rib cage.

Remember, I was playing without glasses or contact lenses. The field was a blur of motion. I had called a routine down-and-out pass play, took the snap, faded back into the pocket, and looked downfield. As usual, the panorama before me was severely blurred, and I paused in the pocket to try to find a receiver. My protection collapsed, and the defensive end hit me from my right side, helmet to helmet, and the linebacker blitzing from my left hit me in the left hip at exactly the same moment. Three ribs on my left side separated, and the breath was knocked out of me.

At my coach's urging, I got to my feet and tried to jog around the practice field. The pain was unbearable, and I told him I could not do it. He responded with great disgust and anger, "If you can't run it out, why don't you just take it on into the locker room and turn in your uniform." As a quarterback, I was obviously expendable.

That moment was the beginning of my life as a golfer.

My football-ending injury was during spring practice. About a month later, my dad suggested I play golf with Ishma Davis, a National Guardsman in his battalion and a former Atlanta amateur golf champion. Dad dropped me off at Candler Park in Atlanta on a perfect May afternoon in 1960 with borrowed clubs from my best friend, Randy Stephens.

"Ish" showed me the proper grip and suggested I use a three wood for my tee shot. I teed the ball up, took a smooth swing, and hit the ball down the middle about 180 yards. Life would never be the same.

L-R Joe Souther, Skip Everitt, 1960 East Atlanta High School teammates

I was smitten. From 1960 to this day, golf has been a game of love/hate, elation/depression, and passionate pursuit. In 1963, our high school golf team won the Atlanta high school championship, and I finished runner-up to a big jock named Sam Wyche. Wyche went on to play college football at Furman University, became a successful pro quarterback, and eventually became an NFL head coach.

I am now in my mid-sixties, and the past is a collage of fond memories and magic moments in some of the Earth's most beautiful places. Golf is truly the greatest game ever played, and I feel blessed to have played it for over fifty years. This book is for all of us who are on the "back nine" of our lives but are unwilling to "turn in our uniforms."

Cancer: Life Happens While You Are Planning for the Future

In the spring of 2008, I was diagnosed with prostate cancer. A week before, I had attained my lifetime lowest golf handicap of 5. In August 2008, I was treated in Jacksonville for nine weeks at the University of Florida Proton Institute. While my results were excellent, the daily treatments took a toll on my strength and timing.

Another Setback

Nearly a year later in the spring of 2009, I suffered a mysterious back and rib injury that simulated broken ribs and compressed lower disks. My game deteriorated rapidly.

My longtime friend and golf buddy, Chuck Dolsak, and I were playing in our regular Wednesday nine-hole "dogfight" at the club, a twilight informal tournament that tees off at 5:30 p.m. in the late spring. We were on the fourth hole, a 540-yard par 5. I had hit a good drive and was preparing to hit my second shot to give me a wedge or less for a third shot. I remember thinking, "I am swinging so well, I am going to turn away from the ball just a bit more and fire through the impact to get the shot within sand wedge or lob wedge range." I made a bigger than usual turn, purposely stayed down on the ball, and swung through the shot with more force than my usual smooth tempo. A searing pain jolted through my right ribcage. The feeling was like someone had pressed a hot iron on my ribs. I could hardly breathe.

That swing and that pain launched a six-month search for the source of the injury and a dramatic downturn in my golf game. By the summer of 2009, I had lost distance, accuracy, and confidence, and my handicap had soared to a 14. The days of posting easy 74s, or on a bad day a 78, were a distant memory. After that fateful day in May, 2009, I rarely broke 90 and posted several personal worst rounds.

The Long Road to Recovery
I had been to several doctors, chiropractors, and physical therapists, with no definitive diagnosis forthcoming. After x-rays, an MRI, and a bone scan, a

rheumatologist declared that I had spondylolisthesis, a condition caused by a lower-back disc moving forward and overriding the disc beneath it. The result is inflammation between the two discs and the possibility of lower-back spasms, ribcage pain, and hip pain. I experienced all of these. Finally, in the spring of 2010, I began to regain my strength and confidence.

While the physical part of the setback was over, the worst was yet to come. My brother-in-law, Randy Davis, invited me to return to Green Valley, Arizona, for his annual member/guest tournament. A year earlier, we had won the championship with relative ease. At the end of the 2010 tournament, we were dead last. His game was in mild decline, and I was at my rock bottom. Though the rib and back pain was completely gone, I was mentally AWOL and lacking a shred of confidence in my skills. We never got off the launch pad. It was embarrassing and a serious wake-up call to action.

Thus, in the late spring of 2010, I stood on the first tee of my home course and thought, "What has happened to me?"

A Plan for Recovery
About this time, I read Jimmy Roberts' excellent book *Breaking the Slump*. Heeding his advice, I undertook the following programs and improvement strategies:

1. I registered for several one-day "net" events for senior golfers through the Florida State Golf Association, a chapter of the United States Golf Association. The reason for doing this will be discussed in detail in Chapter Fourteen, "Periodically Play in an Official Competition."

2. I increased my exercise routine, with an emphasis on core strength. This positively affected my balance, tempo, and concentration.

3. I committed to maintain a weight of 168 to172 pounds.

4. I took a one-day intensive short-game clinic sponsored by the PGA Academy in St. Augustine.

5. I followed PGA teacher John Reger's advice, and I visited GolfTEC in Jacksonville and underwent a three-hour swing analysis. GolfTEC videotapes the session and establishes a website for your practice and review.

6. I followed Arnold Palmer's advice and just slowed down, enjoyed the privilege of being "in the game," and stopped trying to change the swing that had served me so well for fifty years.

INTRODUCTION

When I moved to a new local golf community in 1994, I was in the prime of my consulting business. My handicap was a 10, and I began to make friend-ships and form golf relationships that last to this day.

I also began to notice the social structure of the golf community. In Group One, the most frequent play-ers were the older retirees, sixty-five to eighty years old. Next came Group Two, the competent golf-ers and frequent players, who were in their early- to late-middle years, forty to sixty-five years old. Group Three consisted of the young professionals and par-ents of young children. They were occasional play-ers who had effectively put their golf games on the shelf, while they built their professional careers and became soccer moms and dads.

As I visited other clubs across the country, I found this mixture of golfers to be similar, except in the cases of retirement communities that imposed restrictions on the homeowners' and members' ages. Club and golf association tournaments were predominately populated by Group Two. The aver-age USGA handicap for the men in this group was a 15. The range of handicaps was scratch to 34.

As I played in local tournaments, I began to hear a frequent theme among some of the Group Two players. The message was basically, "When I retire, I'm going to really get my game together and kick your #%@* butts!" But in the large majority of cases, the opposite scenario unfolded. The more the retiree played, the worse he or she scored. Middle-age aches and pains turned into chronic injuries; players gained weight and became discouraged and cynical.

This book challenges the myth of "Retirement = Better Golf." The truth is, "The Inevitable Process of Aging + A Golf-Specific Plan for Physical, Mental, and Social Health = Your Best Golf Ever."

CHAPTER ONE:
Commit to a Better Game

"It took me seventeen years to get three thousand hits in baseball. I did it in one afternoon on the golf course."
—Hank Aaron

Each year for as long as I can remember, I have written personal and professional goals for the coming year. I gave up on "resolutions" a long time ago. Resolutions are grandiose, vague, and many times based on someone else's desire to change our behaviors, attitudes, or beliefs. But goals are realistic, measureable, and trackable. They include a plan of action, a system of accountability, and specific results. Resolutions are wishes; goals are plans for results.

As an example, my golf goal for the coming year is "commit to a better game." The plan for achievement of this goal is specifically explained in the forthcoming seventeen chapters. However, since this goal is emotional, personal, and involves more than just my actions and activities, I want to explain the idea of "commitment."

Note: I strongly suggest that you keep a journal of your "eighteen-hole improvement plan." I believe that the process of writing down goals, plans, thoughts, and feelings is one of the most effective ways to define and reinforce new habits and personal change. On the website **backninebook.com** you will find a link to Allison Lebaron, an artist and designer of classical leather journals. If you have seen the movie *Seven Days in Utopia*, the journal used by the star, an aspiring professional tour player, is one of Allison's creations.

I am going to depend on the wonderful work of Stephen Covey in his bestselling book *The Seven Habits of Highly Effective People* to define "commitment." I had the pleasure of being a member of Dr. Covey's training organization from 1990 to 2004. I served as a facilitator for three of his seminars, "The Seven Habits of Highly Effective People," "First Things First," and "Principle-Centered Leadership." For the last ten of those years I was a master facilitator, a trainer of trainers who taught in our client organizations.

Two basic themes of all the seminars were learning new habits of effectiveness and committing to the daily practice of the principles and methods of personal effectiveness learned in the seminars.

To me, these are just other ways to describe the best outcome of commitment. In our seminars we discussed the importance and difficulty of changing our old ways of thinking and doing. We called our current ways of looking at the world and operating in it "our paradigms." Paradigms are the beliefs and experiences that shape our view of life and how to live it. These paradigms are repeated and eventually become habits.

For our purposes, I will define paradigm in a less than positive light. For many golfers, we hold a paradigm that one must be a natural to possess a satisfying, competent game. This paradigm leads to destructive habits like failing to practice, losing control over our emotions, ignoring the rules, abusing our health, playing with the same old gang day in and day out, and never seeking professional help.

So the goal of "commit to a better game" requires a number of shifts in my current set of paradigms. Covey defines the development of new habits as the intersection of knowledge, skill, and desire. All three components are required to develop new, healthy habits.

For the golfer seeking a better game, "knowledge" may be things like learning the rules of golf, identifying your golf temperament, getting a thorough swing analysis and custom club-fitting, and developing a golf-specific fitness routine.

"Skill" is developing a better game through practice, playing with competent partners, playing challenging courses, and entering USGA or other official tournaments.

"Desire" includes self-discipline regarding practice, fitness, nutrition, and etiquette. Also, since desire is a mental process, I recommend reading one or more of the helpful books about the mental side of the game. A list of these is included on **backnine-book.com.**

The eighteen chapters of *The Back Nine* served as the playbook for restoring my game (and now yours) to a level of respectability. I knew that it was going to take some time. The "law of the harvest" states, "You can't rush the crop." Nor can you cram for better golf and a life of meaning.

Commitment to personal change (a better golf game) is best defined in psychologist William James's four-step process:

- Make up your mind.

- Allow no exceptions.

- Seize the first opportunity.

- Continue it.

Dr. Covey writes in his article "Overcoming the Pull of the Past" the following:

> Breaking away from old habits can be compared to the space shuttle leaving the atmosphere. Most of the energy is spent breaking away from the gravity of the earth. Having overcome earth's gravity and traveling 300 miles above the earth, astronauts suddenly experience an endless range of new possibilities in their weightless environment. Likewise, to overcome the gravity of the past and deeply imbedded habits, we must break out of environmental expectations and social definitions. Once we have a victory over self, we have a huge repertoire of choices.

If Dr. Covey's thoughts are a bit heavy, just think of the famous Walt Kelly cartoon character Pogo, who says, "We have met the enemy, and he is us."

Commitment is first an internal list of promises to oneself and then the development of a visible plan of action to keep these promises.

Summary

- Commit to a goal that will produce dramatic improvement in any area of your life.
- Write the goal and the plan of action in a personal journal.
- Check your goal and action plan once a week.
- Make changes, if necessary, to remove roadblocks to your goal.

CHAPTER TWO:
Assess the Level of Your Current Golf Game

"You must work very hard to become a natural golfer."
—Gary Player

Frankly, the "assess the level of your current game" process can become too complicated. I suggest a simple system for assessing your current level of play.

The PGA Tour keeps over three hundred statistics on each player. About 295 are all but useless for those of us in the six to thirty-six handicap range. I polled my panel of experts, and the following five statistics emerged as helpful indicators for tracking progress on the course. (The number in parentheses after the indicator is the average for players on the Champions Tour in 2010.) These Senior Tour averages are not expectations for us, but merely benchmarks that describe the best in the sport. A few of these merit further definition and description.

1. Driving distance (273.5 yards).

During a practice round, use a rangefinder to mea-sure your drives on two randomly chosen par 5s and par 4s. If you do not have a rangefinder, pace off the drives on foot. If you cannot walk between shots, get a playing companion to pace off the drives.

Ideally, visit your local GolfTEC lab (see Chapter Four) or another testing facility. The initial assess-ment will give you a baseline snapshot of distance for all your clubs. It is possible that you will feel a bit overwhelmed by the various metrics, but only a few are relevant to you and your driving distance. For instance, swing speed, length of "carry" (the distance that your drive goes in the air), roll, and total distance are important.

Unfortunately, many senior golfers believe that swing speed is THE secret to longer drives. In reality, balance, tempo, flexibility, and hitting the ball with a solid strike are ways to increase and maintain dis-tance. My swing speed is eighty-five to ninety miles an hour. A miss-hit produces a total driver distance of about 215 yards. A well-hit drive produces a total driving distance of 245 to 260 yards. As we age, our ability to increase our swing speed diminishes and may produce tension and poor balance, and it may cause injury and shorter driving distance.

Another consideration for the senior golfer and driving distance is the length of the driver shaft. The golf-shop racks are full of drivers that have shafts that measure forty-five to forty-seven inches. The old standard length for drivers is 44.5 inches. Again, I went to my panel of experts and a recent video from the Golf Channel for advice. The verdict: Shorter is better. Master golf fitter Ricky Strain builds drivers for seniors with two key features: a forty-two- to forty-three-inch shaft and eleven to fourteen degrees of loft.

Note: When I am playing a lot of golf, my distance invariably increases. By playing, practicing, and working on balance and core strength (Pilates), my tempo and focus allow me to swing through the ball with confidence.

Good Tempo + Confidence + The Right Driver for You = Longer, Straighter Drives.

2. Driving accuracy (70.1 percent hit fairways).

Hitting fairways is a guaranteed way to increase your chance for a par or bogey (or better). If you play courses with a short rough and few trees, an errant drive may not be punitive. However, on better courses or tree-lined courses, a drive that lands in the rough may create a one- to three-shot increase in the score for the hole. My home course has narrow, tree-lined fairways on literally every hole. The quality of your driving accuracy on our course can easily make a six- to twelve-stroke difference per round.

The principles of driving accuracy are the same as for driving distance.

The number-one reason for an errant drive is "steering," or trying to guide the ball down the fairway. Once again, good balance, smooth tempo, and a lack of tension will produce drives that are both longer and straighter.

3. Greens in regulation (65.4 percent).

Hitting greens in regulation gives you a chance at a birdie, par, or at worst, bogey. Obviously, long and accurate drives set you up for the possibility of hitting the green. Personally, I have increased my greens in regulation (GIR) by adding two hybrids to my set of clubs. These "game improvement" clubs take the place of my former number-four and number-five irons.

One additional strategy is for you to "get real" about your distances for each club. Ten years ago, I could hit a nine iron 150 yards. Today the seven iron is a better bet to get the ball on the green from that same yardage. As with driving distance, you can measure the average distance for each club with a range finder, by pacing off your distances, or by using a fitting lab.

I am willing to bet that most of your failures to hit a green in regulation are shots that end up short of the green. Keep a mental note of your misses. How many were short of the green? How many were too long? My guess is that 90 percent of your shots that missed the greens are short, and 10 percent are too long.

4. Putts per round (32.4).

My wife calls the corner of the garage where I store my golf equipment the "putter museum." I have every kind of putter made except for a "broomstick" or long putter. When I have a good day and score well, you can assume that I had twenty-eight to thirty-two putts. Even on a bad day, if you are putting well, your score will most likely be respectable. If you are plagued by three-putts, missed four-footers, or constant misreads of greens, consult a professional.

5. Scrambling (up and downs for par, 67 percent).

Can you remember your best round ever? Most likely it included some great "up and down" moments, chip-ins, and sand saves. How about memories of some of your nightmare rounds? Do the terms "chilly dip," "fat," "skull," "fluff," and "blade" sound familiar? Watch the pros on TV on a tournament Sunday. Hundreds of thousands of dollars are gained or lost from one hundred yards or less to the hole.

My advice? Yes, another lesson from a pro and hours of practice. In addition, pay particular attention to the advice of Lynn Marriott and Pia Nillson.

The authors of *Play Your Best Golf Now* advise us to assess the best shot to attempt (the Thought Box) and then step up to the ball and execute the shot (the Play Box).

Personally, the chipping aspect of the game is a constant challenge for me. When I am relaxed, focused, and confident, I literally believe I can hole out chips or get them to "inside the leather" on any hole.

Note: I have designed a simple, pocket-sized, on-course Improvement Tracker for your use on the course. You will find it online at **backninebook.com**. It is a printable form about the size of a checkbook. Put it under your scorecard or in your back pocket and keep it current from hole to hole. After the round, you will be able to assess your on course performance and set up a practice routine to improve any areas that need work.

Summary

- Pay attention to and track the five metrics for improvement: driving distance, driving accuracy, greens in regulation, putts per round, and scrambling.
- Go to **backninebook.com** and print a few of the Improvement Trackers. Start using them immediately and review each round to identify parts of your game that need improvement.

CHAPTER THREE:
Set Realistic Goals for Improvement

"I have always had a drive that pushed me to try for perfection, and golf is a game in which perfection stays just out of reach."
—Betsy Rawls

Now the hard part begins. I am going to share with you *my* specific annual goals in three areas. Why just three? Our brain's ability to implement more than three goals at a time is limited. Since I am guaranteeing that you will develop and maintain a better game, I want to use the power of focus to limit goals to a manageable three. I am not suggesting that these must be *your* goals. You may choose a completely different set of improvement targets, based on your individual physical fitness, skill, and experience level.

Goal Number One
Increase the value of every one of the five metrics listed in Chapter Two by 10 percent.

For instance, if my current driving distance is 220 yards, my goal is to do what it takes to increase this distance to 242 yards. The tactics and routine for achieving a 10 percent increase in driver distance are imbedded in the following chapters and include a fitting for a new driver, core-strength and flexibility training, and an emphasis on increasing swing speed within my limits of staying in balance.

For the driver fitting, I will go to GolfTEC in Jacksonville. It is a national franchise, so I expect a GolfTEC facility to be within your reach. It is a great value—seventy dollars for the basic analysis—and GolfTEC is an independent lab with no bias toward any club manufacturer.

For the core-strength and balance part of the goal, I will interview Shannon Foley, owner of Encore Pilates, and continue my twice-a-week practice of Pilates at her studio, as well as increase my home workout routine.

I will build a similar plan for every one of the five improvement metrics from Chapter Two. For this goal to be valid and effective, I will need to set a timeline and end date for each metric. For driving distance, I have chosen ninety days to create the increase in distance from 220 to 242.

Goal Number Two
Play in one competitive event each month.

This is a realistic and achievable goal for me for two reasons. First, I live in Florida and am a member of the Florida State Golf Association. The FSGA sponsors dozens of one- to four-day events statewide for players of all ages and abilities. Second, I am a member of my country club's men's golf association and have additional opportunities to play in their events and in the club championships.

Goal Number Three

Keep my health, fitness, and skills in good shape even during times of travel, bad weather, or work assignments.

For me, this goal is crucial for maintaining the progress made by achieving goals number one and number two. Historically, my golf game has suffered when laziness took over during a long business trip, a spell of cold weather, or a family vacation. The secret to avoid losing my hard-earned progress is to keep up the exercise, nutrition, and golf-specific learning even during times when a real golf course or practice facility is not available. As we age, this goal grows in difficulty AND importance.

In Chapter Six, Shannon Foley will offer some great advice about how to stay fit in all challenging situations. I will give you a hint: take a TheraBand everywhere you go. TheraBand is a rubber elastic band about eight inches wide and six feet long. You can simulate a full free-weight and stretching routine with this one simple device anywhere, anytime. It is packable, weighs only a few ounces, and is inexpensive. More on the TheraBand in Chapter Six.

I am betting that you have noticed that the mere three goals I have set are full of required activities and new or strengthened habits. But because I am fully committed to a better game of golf (Chapter One) throughout the rest of my playing days, these activities and habits are mandatory for success.

Summary

- Become committed, mentally and physically, to a better game.
- Use a system to measure improvement in five critical areas of your current game.
- Write three specific, realistic, attainable goals that will ensure success during the coming year.

CHAPTER FOUR:
Seek Professional Help

"You can't see your own backswing."
—Anonymous

Swing Analysis and Club Fitting

For better or for worse, many of the swing-analysis and club-fitting facilities have a "dog in the hunt" in terms of a bias toward one brand of club. I recommend GolfTEC for several reasons. They are unbiased and will provide data that can be used to demo several brands of clubs. Their initial analysis is around seventy dollars, a very reasonable price for a thorough analysis. Your analysis goes to a website that only you can access so that you can review the session and your professional's comments. GolfTEC uses multiple cameras and a sensor vest to record a variety of swing factors.

Many of us have avoided the swing-analysis and club-fitting process for a variety of reasons. We chose our clubs based on price, the recommendations of others, or the popularity of a certain brand among our touring heroes. We learn to play pretty well with these clubs through adapting our swing to the loft, lie, kick point, shaft, and bounce of these clubs. As any pro will tell you, a swing analysis and club fitting are essential for game improvement or maintenance.

There is not a scratch amateur or touring professional who uses off-the-shelf equipment. In our later years, our swing speed, flexibility, balance, and hand/eye coordination go through changes. If you really want to play your best golf ever as a senior, make the investment in a reputable analysis and a set of clubs that match your swing. This game is difficult enough. Get the right clubs for your current level of physical fitness and enjoy a new level of satisfaction with your game. By the way, a good lab like GolfTEC will fit you for every club in the bag, including wedges and putter.

What Is in My Bag?

At the time of writing this book, my set consists of the following clubs and accessories:

- *Driver.* Ping G10 10.5-degree loft, forty-two-inch Accra XT60 shaft. Master club fitter Ricky Strain of Precision Golf built my driver. He is a strong advocate of higher loft and shorter-length shafts for the senior player. Both my driving distance and accuracy are steadily improving.

- *Three wood.* Cleveland seventeen degree.

- *Five wood.* TaylorMade Burner nineteen degree.

- *Hybrids.* Twenty-one- and twenty-six-degree Cleveland Mashies.

- *Irons.* Six through P Cleveland CG sixteen with R shafts. These irons are my first custom-fitted ones and were built online on the Srixon/Cleveland Golf website. They have given me both distance and spin-rate gains.

- *Wedges.* Cleveland forty-eight-degree gap wedge, 54 degree sand wedge and 62 degree lob wedge.

- *Putter.* During the last year, I have alternated between a 2008 Rife Two Bar belly putter and a 1996 Odyssey Rossi 2 Dual Force mallet. The belly putter seems to be an antidote to the occasional yips, but the Rossi consistently reduces putts per round when I am putting well.

Technology WILL Improve Your Game

Do you remember the first time you hit one of the "new" clubs? I was in Southern California on a combined work-and-golf trip in 1991 and stayed in a hotel near a local driving range. The day I arrived was "demo day" for a club called the Big Bertha. The Callaway rep suggested I tee the ball a bit higher than usual and play the ball off my left instep. To my amazement, my first swing produced the longest drive I had ever hit! The leap in technology by Callaway Golf changed my game forever. At that time, I had Hogan Speed Slot woods, Macgregor Tommy Armour irons, and a Bull's-eye putter.

Summary

- Get an analysis of your current swing. I recommend GolfTEC Learning Centers.
- Update your equipment. Consider investing in custom-fitted clubs, especially your driver, hybrids, and mid to short irons.

CHAPTER FIVE:
Practice with a Purpose—
And Have Fun

"Insanity: Doing the same thing over and over again and expecting different results."
—*Albert Einstein*

In the introduction, I told the story of my first round of golf at Candler Park in Atlanta. Shortly after that fateful day in May, I began to hang around the clubhouse and caddie shack. Eventually the pro at Candler, Jim Yates, asked me to "loop" for him in exchange for lessons. I carried his and another player's bags around the hilly nine-hole municipal course for fifty cents per player. After the round, "Chick" (Jim's nickname) would drive me in his private golf cart down to the #6 fairway, a long par 4 with enough room for a practice tee near the creek. Some days I would shag several bags of practice balls for the pro, and then he would give me a lesson. The swing I have today, fifty years later, is basically the swing that Chick Yates taught me. He also taught me several new cuss words and regaled me with tales of a life lived fast and furious. While he was never successful as a touring pro, Chick was known all over the golf galaxy as a good teacher, a savvy gambler, and an aficionado of multiple vices. I was lucky to know him and to enjoy the game of golf because of his coaching and encouragement.

Along the way, I took periodic lessons from pros in whichever city I lived. One of the best teachers I have ever had is Pete Dunham, head golf professional at Snee Farm in Mt. Pleasant, South Carolina. I met Pete when he was on the team of PGA professionals that opened the Haile Plantation Golf and Country Club in Gainesville in 1994. About a year later he founded, built, and became part owner of the Gainesville Golf Practice Facility. Pete has a true passion for teaching others, and even PGA and LPGA professionals seek him out for help. Unlike many of the teachers I have employed, Pete is truly student-centered and believes that learning the game of golf requires science, psychology, the appropriate attitude, fitness, and dedication. He has also been inside the ropes as caddie for his wife, Jean Marie Busuttil, LPGA professional and player on both the Futures and LPGA tour.

I asked Pete to discuss the way he approaches a senior golfer during lessons and to define a plan of practice for readers of *The Back Nine*. Specifically, I asked him to reflect on how a serious senior golfer can improve his or her game with proper practice. Here is his advice:

First of all, practice in a manner that fights the natural tendency to be more stable. The fear of falling as we age, due to functional degradation, begins the steady decline in consistency and power for most golfers.

Second, swinging a golf club is a dynamic motion, using force and counterforce optimally. Practice in a manner that allows you to use these dynamic forces freely and fully. Practice to build and improve your balance and equilibrium at the end of your swing. Hold the finish five to ten seconds. Stretching the finish will move you farther into a fully rotated, relaxed, balanced finish while you are hanging out in that position.

The best balance drill that Pete taught me is the one-legged drill. As you improve, swing harder while maintaining balance. Take your normal stance and then move your right foot behind your left foot, with your right toe pointing downward. Swing and gently sweep the right foot around to its normal position. Easier said than done!

Pete adds the following:

Last, practice in a manner that keeps you from over-stabilizing. With or without a ball, swing the club into balance with your feet in motion. I call it the step-through drill. It is often referred to as the "baseball drill." Start with your feet together. As you begin the swing, build the natural rhythm of a throw by stepping and swinging into balance. This is great to do without a golf ball because it will override the strike instinct in the swing as well as push out that pesky need for stability as you continue to train in motion.

Pete's approach to teaching the game of golf is based on the theories and practices in David Lee's book *Gravity Golf*. The main idea of Lee's approach is to practice awkward and off-balance setups and golf swings. It is a counterintuitive approach that will make you very uncomfortable in the beginning. I highly suggest that you read Lee's book and study the illustrations for his set of unorthodox drills.

The drills described above—the one-legged drill and the step-through drill—are two of the most effective drills that a golfer struggling with ball-striking problems can use.

How I Practice

As I wrote this book, two of my favorite golf writers, Lynn Marriott and Pia Nillson, had just published *The Game Before the Game*. Their approach is closely aligned with the practice routines suggested by Pete Dunham. I hold their writing in high regard and find their approach to the mental side of the game to be easily understood and implemented. If you combine the writings of Dunham, Marriott, Nillson, Bob Rotella, and even Bobby Jones, a pattern of basic rules of practice emerge. Use the following as your "How to Practice" checklist.

Summary

- Warm up before every practice session. My ideal warm-up is twelve minutes on my stationary bike, a few snow angels on my Pilates foam roll, two or three yoga poses (e.g., cobra, downward dog, cat stretch), and ten full squats with a TheraBand stretched and held over my head like a barbell. All this takes less than twenty minutes and gets me ready to hit the range running and reduces the likelihood of injury.
- Practice with purpose. Hit every shot with a goal in mind.
- Emphasize the short game. Become familiar with the distances of each of your wedges.
- Adopt several of the well-known putting drills from the books of Dave Pelz or Phil Mickelson.
- Practice hitting the ball from awkward stances, off balance, with feet close together, opposite-handed, with eyes closed, and any other way that defies the conventional golf swing.
- Simulate holes that you will play on the course while you are on the range. I usually simulate the opening par 4 by hitting driver, nine iron, and—just in case—a chip with my fifty-six-degree wedge. I then move on to the second hole and tee up an eight iron. If I have time, I will simulate playing three to

six holes that require a variety of clubs and shots.

- Use alignment sticks to check your core rotation, setup, and target alignment, and also as a putting track on the practice green.
- Review your Improvement Tracker from your most recent round. Work on the shots that cost you strokes. How many putts did you take? Were your misses consistent? Were your long-lag putts creating difficult second (or third) putts? Then off you go to the practice green! Were your iron shots mostly "chunks" or other mis-hits? Then practice the one-legged drill described earlier in this chapter. Were a wide variety of your shots poorly executed? Then read the section from Marriott and Nillson's book *Play Your Best Golf Now* that describes the Think Box and the Play Box as a way to restore focus and concentration.
- Go back to the foreword of this book and reread Tom Jenkins's advice about the importance of physical fitness and the short game.

A Note of Caution

Marriot, Nillson, and Jenkins remind us that overpractice, or practicing to the point of extreme fatigue, is counterproductive. The practice routine described above can take all day or as little as ninety minutes total, including stretching. Check your level of energy as you prepare for practice. Some days call for brief tune-ups, and other days are perfect for that long, well-planned, comprehensive practice session. Also, few of us can or should practice every day. Some days are for playing with our buddies, playing in a competitive tournament, or just roaming a few fairways in the waning light of the day as a single. And even though we avid golfers are reluctant to admit it, some days are just for living the other parts of our lives!

CHAPTER SIX:
Adopt a Golf-Specific Fitness Routine

"There was a time when the high school quarter-back wouldn't dare admit he played golf. Now the high school quarterback is no longer a quarter-back—he's a golfer."
—Nathaniel Welch

"You met your wife in Pilates? I didn't know she was European!"
—TV commercial about NFL tailgating

The Core of Better Senior Golf
Pilates is truly the core of good health.

In a February 2009 *Mayo Clinic Health Letter*, the concept of core stability was defined and described as the following: "Your core—the area around your trunk—houses your center of gravity, supports your spine, and stabilizes you." Developing core stability is the number-one way to combat poor posture and lower-back pain. Core stability is achieved through floor exercises, the practice of Pilates, and the use of fitness balls. Of these three, Pilates is rapidly becoming the gold standard of core stability for the senior golfer.

The method known as Pilates is named after the late Joseph Pilates (1880–1967), a German expatriate who developed a series of exercises during World War I to help former prisoners of war regain their strength and flexibility. Stott Pilates best represents the modern version of the Pilates approach. I strongly suggest you go to **www.stottpilates.com** for more information.

I recently interviewed Shannon Foley, owner of Encore Pilates in Gainesville, Florida. Shannon is a certified Stott Pilates expert and a physical therapist. My wife, Lynda, and I have been students of Shannon's for ten years. Shannon has guided us through injuries, age-related flexibility issues, and day-to-day health issues. Lynda and I are, to put it mildly, raving fans of Pilates and particularly thankful to Shannon for her sensitivity to our specific health issues.

Here is the heart of our interview:

Q: What do you see as differences between the thirty-five-year-old Pilates student/golfer and the senior Pilates student and golfer?

A: The senior student must concentrate on longer warm-up sessions before a round of golf and focus the warm-up on flexibility. Flexibility enables the senior to retain the rotation of the spine necessary for a powerful and controlled golf swing. In the absence of proper rotation, we tend to "slide" instead of rotate. Our core movement from side to side causes a variety of poor outcomes. The sliding of our core forward or backward can cause blocked shots to the right or those famous "duck hooks" that cost us many strokes over the course of a round of golf.

Q: My swing seems to get shorter and slower each year. What can I do to regain my former club-head speed and flexibility?

A: Losing flexibility and swing speed is a natural consequence of aging. Accepting these facts of life will enable you to maintain your current level of strength and flexibility through Pilates, yoga, and resistance exercises. Don't forget the value of walking, swimming, and constantly being aware of your "flexion," or posture. The "senior slump" is mostly due to poor posture, a sedentary lifestyle, and lack of exercise. Poor posture leads to back pain, fatigue, and a permanent weak core.

Q: How does a novice get started with Pilates?

A: The first and most critical step is to get a baseline evaluation from a certified Pilates practitioner. Choose your Pilates practitioner carefully, ask to see his or her credentials, and ask for long-term references from clients. A thorough baseline evaluation takes about ninety minutes and provides the

Pilates practitioner with the information to design a customized program for you. Without this evaluation, you risk injury or the development of poor technique at the hands of a questionable personal trainer.

Q: So what is the "magic bullet" for maintaining maximum flexibility and good health?

A: The Mayo Clinic actually uses the term "magic bullet" to describe the benefits of developing core stability, preventing disease, increasing life expectancy, and increasing personal energy. I would add gentle yoga, walking, biking, and swimming as endurance exercises. Last, I would carefully examine my diet and add a nutritionist to my list of coaches.

Note: This chapter on fitness may be the most important of all. Personally, I have successfully been treated for cancer, endured attacks of back and neck issues over the years, and recovered each time. I credit the expert coaching of supportive professionals like Shannon Foley, Jenna Robinson, Valerie Owens, Trish Gregory, Pete Dunham, Mike Chance, and numerous yoga practitioners. In other words, it takes a village to be as good as you can be as you age. I consider the experts listed above to be essential coaches, friends, and resources.

Speaking of support, I would be remiss if I did not list my wife, Lynda, as the "offensive coordinator" (to borrow language from football) of this coaching staff. Her encouragement, role modeling, and unrelenting support make all this planning, exercise, and mindfulness worthwhile. Actually, she nagged me into starting Pilates. God bless her.

In the introduction, I mentioned TheraBands as portable fitness aids for the serious senior golfer. For information on ordering Therabands and how to use these simple devices, go to **www.backninebook. com**

Summary

- Begin or renew a golf-specific exercise routine.
- Make Pilates the center of your exercise routine.
- Keep your exercise routine simple and fun.

CHAPTER SEVEN:
Develop Stamina and Focus through Better Nutrition

"The biggest technological advance in golf in the next fifty years will not be equipment or exercise. It will be nutrition."
—*Gary Player*

I asked nutritionist Tricia Gregory to comment on the challenges of aging, nutrition, and fitness. Specifically, I asked her to comment on "golf course food," supplements, and an ideal daily diet for older athletes. Here are her comments:

Q: As athletes grow older, what dietary mistakes do you see them make that eventually become barriers to performance?

A: Many older athletes think that an increase in vegetarian meals will contribute to their performance in any sport. I agree with increasing the portions of fresh fruits and vegetables, but would advise any older people to make sure they are getting enough protein.

Q: We older golfers tend to eat out frequently. How do we choose wisely from a restaurant menu or a buffet to maintain our commitment to better nutrition? The golf course grill and bar are seldom sources of healthy food.

A: If there are a group of golfers who regularly eat at the course dining facility, they should make an appointment with the chef or manager (usually 2:00 p.m. is the best time to catch a food-service person) and have two or three specific choices that they would like the chef or manager to consider.

If a golfer is visiting a course, usually the best options are soups, grilled meat or fish with a baked potato, and steamed vegetables. Also, consider sandwiches made with whole-grain bread, and choose lean meat or vegetarian fillings. Sometimes if a healthy entrée is not available, a baked potato and a side or two will be the best option. To set your appetite at a lower level, eat a piece of fruit or an energy bar during the round.

Q: Are you a fan of supplements? If so, which ones are best for seniors?

A: Supplements will not make up for a bad diet, but they do help to fill in the gaps. A standard one-a-day, recognized-brand vitamin/mineral supplement is your best bet. The large name-brand supplements are subject to rigorous quality control that minimizes the chance of inappropriate amounts of some vitamins or minerals.

Q: Will you outline an ideal diet for a day for a senior athlete, specifically a golfer?

A: I will refer you to one. Go to **www.caloriecontrol. org** and click on "Recipes for a Healthy Lifestyle," then "2,000 Calories a Day the Healthy Way." Also, if you want a customized nutritional plan, go to **www. wellnesscoaches.com.** Please consult your primary physician before adopting a two-thousand-calorie diet. Your caloric needs may vary substantially with age or exercise levels.

I know that it will be difficult for many of us to break away from the "meat and potatoes" routine that we have practiced since childhood, but it sounds like the benefits of Trisha Gregory's recommendations will increase our focus, raise our energy, and extend our stamina.

Summary

- Maintain a healthy, athletic diet by making good decisions about which foods and what amounts are appropriate.
- Practice portion control that produces an appropriate number of calories per day and you may be rewarded with increased energy and loss of excess weight.

CHAPTER EIGHT:
Play the Course, Get off the Range

"The hardest putt you will ever have is the eight-footer that, if you miss it, you don't have enough money to pay off your bet."
—*Skip Everitt*

I included my own quotation here because I can still remember my shaking hands and the feeling of emptiness in my stomach as I crouched over an eight-foot putt on the ninth green at Candler Park golf course in Atlanta in the summer of 1960. Up until that eight-foot putt, I had spent that summer playing golf and caddying for my boss and teaching professional, Jim "Chick" Yates. Late that summer, Chick invited me to play in his regular foursome. I had only played golf about a year and had never placed a wager or bet on any round or part of the game. Thus, when Chick suggested a two-dollar Nassau, I was too embarrassed to decline and said yes.

Our foursome was made up of Chick Yates, a member of the PGA for twenty-five years; his son, Wayne Yates, a PGA touring pro; "Rabbit" Johnson, a forty-five-year-old fulltime caddy who could drive the green on Candler Park's longest hole, a 425-yard par 4; and me, a fifteen-year-old high school golfer who had yet to break 40 for nine holes.

As luck would have it, I drew Wayne Yates as my playing partner. After a shaky start, I made a few pars. A par on number nine would give me a 39 for the round, and Wayne and I could halve our match. The ninth hole is a short, uphill par 4 with a small, flat green. All four of us hit the green with our second shots. Of the foursome, I had the shortest putt—an eight-foot, downhill, right-to-left, fast-breaking monster. One by one the three fine golfers before me missed their putts. At this point, Wayne and I were tied with our competitors. That is when I remembered that I had less than a dollar in my pocket. I had heard the stories of losers who did not pay their debts immediately after the round. Rarely were they ever invited to play again.

I read the putt like a pro, walked up to the ball, took a deep breath, and put a great stroke on the putt. I did not look up, but I heard one chuckle and two groans as the ball disappeared into the hole. At that moment I remembered a quotation from Bobby Jones's great book, *Bobby Jones on Golf*. To paraphrase, "There is golf, and then there is competitive golf. The two are very different."

Perhaps I should have saved this story for the chapter on betting and competition. However, for me this day was about more than just making and keeping bets. It was about playing on the course, not the practice range. It was about the adrenaline and the elation that comes from playing the best that you have ever played. You can hit a thousand balls on the practice range and never call it your best round. A 39 on your scorecard and a win in your four-ball match are truly priceless.

The pros do it, we did it as younger players, and those flat-bellied fifteen-year-olds do it every day. Go out and play! I know a guy at my club who is almost paranoid about actually playing our course. He is a perfectionist and believes that he is rarely ready or worthy to play a round of golf or even a few holes at the end of the day. I believe that it is important, healthy, and fun to balance practice and play. His unwillingness to leave the practice range and just PLAY has made him a pretty miserable person whose golf game is not appreciably better for all his ball pounding.

Time on the range is very important, but it is an incomplete practice experience. Time on the range leaves out course management, creativity, and situation management. When you are actually on a real golf course, the GAME of golf is in play, not just the mechanics of the swing. I have attended many PGA and amateur tournaments and probably gained the most personal benefit from attending a practice round.

Several years ago during such a practice round at a PGA tour event, I followed David Duval and Tommi Tolles for over three hours. They were both at the pinnacle of their games. None of the holes they played were straight up. They would hit two or three tee shots, one or two fairway approaches, and then went to work from one hundred yards in to learn the angles and bounces around each green. In addition, they played a variation of the basket-ball game H-O-R-S-E. David would drop a ball in the knurliest rough he could find near the green, hit his shot, and then Tommi would hit from the same spot. Closest to the pin won the bet. This would go on for five to ten minutes on each hole. While their game of H-O-R-S-E appeared playful and relaxed, the knowledge they gained about the course and the state of their short games could have been the difference between making the cut on Friday, and a great payday on Sunday, or a long ride back to Atlanta on Friday empty-handed.

So when you find yourself on a course with nobody behind you, let the "kid" out and drop some balls in a variety of awkward, difficult, and challenging places that require creativity, imagination, and even a good old "trick shot."

PGA-certified teacher Pete Dunham requires that part of every practice, whether on the course or on the range, includes creating lies and situations that test our balance, tempo, and creativity. Can you hit a ball backward? Can you hit a ball from the opposite side of your normal way? Can you hit a successful shot from a divot? When you practice sand shots, do you include "fried eggs" and twenty- to fifty-yard blasts? Do you practice hitting from fairway bunkers? Can you hit a ball under overhanging limbs? I think you get my point. A golf course is made up of beautifully manicured fairways and greens surrounded by sand, water, trees, brush, cactus, and deep rough. We all know that we will have multiple opportunities to hit from challenging lies on every round. So have fun practicing worst-case scenarios.

Summary

- Remember that a real golf course is the best place to practice strategy, shot making, and "feel."
- Practice like the professionals—create a game or two that turns up the pressure to improve.
- Play parts of the course that are most difficult. Get dirty! Learn to hit a ball out of sand, water (à la Bill Haas!), waste areas, deep rough, and other terrible, horrible, no-good situations.

CHAPTER NINE:
Raise the Bar for Your Game by Playing with Three Levels of Partners

"The simple truth is that golfers can be divided into learners and nonlearners. Whether you are a learner or nonlearner is up to you."
—James Ragonnet, *Golf's Three Noble Truths*

One of the big mistakes I see as a golfer ages is for him or her to play only "buddy" golf everyday. I am not at all against playing with a regular group of friends for most of your rounds, but a dose of variety is needed to improve and maintain one's game. The tendency I have observed among buddy groups is that members are at about the same level of skill and scoring. Perhaps we feel threatened by the younger flat-belly who outdrives us by thirty to sixty yards on every par 4 and par 5. Or maybe it is the intimidation factor of playing against a senior player with a scratch handicap left over from his playing days on a college team, the PGA tour, and a stint as a college golf coach.

My friend and neighbor John Darr played and coached at all these levels and is a treat (or threat) to play against. Also, you can count on him to help you in any way to improve your game. While we average-to-good seniors are elated with our best-ever rounds of 74 to 77, he calmly hits green after green, makes a boatload of putts, and goes home after the two-day club senior championship with rounds in the high to mid-60s. I always learn something from John Darr's methods, experience, and abilities. (See his comments in the appendix of this book.)

So wrangle your way into a situation from time to time to play along with the club or course champion or the up-and-coming high school player who has just been offered a golf scholarship to Texas A&M or Western Carolina University. Three levels of golfing partners—a peer, a very good amateur, and a professional—will all help raise your level of play.

As a real stretch, play with an active PGA professional at least once a year. I am truly lucky to be a member of a club where the resident professionals frequently play casual matches with members, and even take us on outings to other courses as teammates. Somewhere along their life journey they have played at a highly competitive level—as a club or course professional—and consider it a win-win to get to know members on the course. If this is not possible for you, take an on-course lesson from a local class-A PGA professional. *(A note to all spouses and other family members of the reader of this book: An on-course lesson is a great birthday/ holiday present for the avid senior player.)*

As my game improved, I decided to book an on-course lesson with my club's first assistant golf professional, Tommi Ylijoki. It was a terrific experience, and I want to share the on-course issues we addressed, which were the following:

1. Tommi checked my alignment on every shot for our fourth hole, a long par 5. He pointed out that my alignment was consistently to the right of my target. I had no idea that this was true. I could not see the alignment problem. He suggested something that was an instant fix for the alignment issue. It was not a new idea, but it was one I had forgotten over the years. To improve your alignment, create a pre-shot routine that includes picking a target, then finding a secondary target about a foot in front of your ball. Swing through this secondary target, and you will be amazed by the accuracy of your shot.

2. We found certain areas of the course that were "stroke eaters." For me, the deep, wiry rough adjacent to some of our elevated greens was the source of frequent chunks, chilly dips, and skulled lob shots that added one or more strokes to the hole. This shot was particularly damaging when I short-sided my approach, leaving me with little or no chance of scrambling for par. Tommi suggested

that I redefine the shot by using the same swing as if I were in a bunker. I opened the face of my sixty-degree wedge and made my usual sand-shot swing. The ball popped up and onto the green and landed like a snowflake two feet from the hole!

3. We next stopped at an area of waste under an overhanging live oak. The green was elevated, but there was no shot possible that would carry the green. To add to the misery, heavy rough hugging the fringe complicated the option of a bump and run. Now things got a bit tricky. Tommi's advice was to hit an area in front of the green that would create a big first bounce and produce a shot that found the green while avoiding a runner through the rough. In essence, I hit the ball a bit harder than usual and aimed for the knoll of rough in front of me. The result was that the ball took one big bump, landed on the fringe, rolled to the hole, hit the pin, and settled about six feet away. Par!

4. We played number five, a 195-yard uphill par 3. Check alignment, pick an intermediate target in front of the ball, have a nice slow backswing, and fire through the ball. High, hard five wood, pin high, twenty feet away. Done.

5. We moved on to the number-six tee, our number-one handicap hole and a 540-yard par 5. I asked Tommi, "How do you get a little extra distance during a match on a long hole like this?" His advice

was to tee the ball slightly higher than usual, step a bit closer to the ball, and concentrate on hitting the ball as solidly as possible. He emphasized the importance of balance and tempo, not a faster swing. This advice created an instant improvement in distance and accuracy.

The bottom line of this sidebar is not that I achieved miraculous results instantly (although I did in some cases), but that this on-course lesson was the right thing to do, at the right time and in a real-time situation. An on-course lesson is most effective when your basic swing is working. The on-course lesson is about shot making, strategy, and gaining confidence.

A Warning

Frankly, I am not addressing this chapter to the corporate CEO or celebrity who plays at Pebble Beach every year with the touring pros by paying a mega-bucks sponsor fee. I am talking to the thousands of dedicated senior golfers who want to walk the course with a player who has tour-level experience, for a reasonable cost.

A Final Note

Watching the best players in person is fun, helpful, and inspiring. Do not let your golfing life end before you attend a PGA/LPGA tournament. Do not wait for a major to come to your area. Attend *any* tour event, pick a favorite player, and follow him for his entire round, or park your folding chair on a great golf hole and watch the field pass through. Personally, I have attended the Masters twice, the U.S. Open once, and the Players Championship fifteen times. Frankly, my most intimate and enjoyable tournaments were the three nationwide tournaments played in my hometown on a course that I play two to three times a year. The year before the tournament moved to another city, I served as a starter at the first and tenth holes. What a thrill to meet and chat with many of the players as they endeavored to qualify for the big tour.

Summary

- Have a group of regular golf buddies.
- Expand your golf opportunities to include highly skilled amateurs and professionals.
- Schedule an on-course lesson with your teacher.
- Attend a PGA/LPGA event each year. Observe how the professionals practice, play, and conduct themselves.

CHAPTER TEN:
Know the Rules of Golf

"You may as well praise a man for not robbing a bank as to praise him for playing by the rules."
—Bobby Jones, after being complimented on his sportsmanship

"I have come to think that a person grows in his regard for the rules as he improves his game. The best players come to love golf so much they hate to see it violated in any way."
—Michael Murphy, Golf in the Kingdom

"It is unbelievable how much you don't know about the game you've been playing all your life."
—Mickey Mantle

In 2011 my wife, Lynda, and I attended the one-day rules workshop sponsored by the USGA and the Florida State Golf Association. In 2012, I attended the three day USGA rules workshop in Las Vegas The experiences were exhausting, sometimes confusing, and eminently worthwhile. I want to stake a claim or justification for every golfer to take this workshop.

I GUARANTEE you that knowledge of the rules of golf will make you a better player, a supportive playing partner, and an asset to your course or club.

As I wrote this book I was moving the process forward to become a certified USGA rules official. There is a huge message in this chapter for senior players regarding the rules of golf. As our playing abilities decline, we can stay in the game as volunteers and rules officials at a variety of tournaments. We can serve on our men's or women's tournament-rules committee. If we are willing to invest the time and effort, we can serve as officials for USGA, high school, college, and PGA tour events. Think about it as you plan the later stages of your life as a golfer. Join your state golf association, take the workshop, and get "inside the ropes" to contribute to the game as a volunteer.

There is great value in knowing the rules as a player. Knowledge of the rules can save you strokes, help your partners and competitors play better, and establish you as a source of knowledge for your course or club. Carry the official rulebook in your bag or download the rules as an app on your smartphone. When in doubt during competitive play, call the pro and ask for an interpretation.

As a player, you will find yourself in situations where the proper interpretation of the rules of golf will determine whether you are permitted relief from a seemingly unplayable position or lie. In addition, you can avoid penalty strokes or the loss of the hole in match-play situations, and avoid disqualification in competitive events. Most of us senior players know the handful of most likely situations that require strict adherence to an official golf rule (e.g., grounding your club in a hazard, playing the wrong ball, failing to replace your ball after moving it out of another player's line on the green, hitting out of turn, or hitting a ball out of bounds). Even in these most common situations, however, there are exceptions, and the one-day workshop combined with your course professional's knowledge will help to sort out the more unusual decisions.

Socially, it is no fun to play golf with someone who lacks knowledge of the rules, or worse, abuses or ignores them during even a casual round. I will not mince words on this topic. To abuse or ignore the rules of golf is to cheat—period.

A Cautionary Note
Resist becoming the "rules troll" in your "friendly game" group. Be of assistance to others through diplomatic role-modeling and gentle reminders to others about a rules situation or exception. Be a teacher, not a pompous enforcer.

Knowing the rules of golf signifies that you are both a player and a student of the greatest game. In your later years, your knowledge of, and passion for, the rules of golf may provide you with a way to stay connected to this game for a lifetime.

Summary

- Read the rules of golf and keep a copy in your golf bag or as an app on your smartphone. Many players also have a copy of the USGA book, *Golf Rules Illustrated*, as a visual resource.
- Attend a one-day rules workshop sponsored by your state golf association or the USGA.
- Consider becoming a volunteer for your local USGA, state golf association, or high school tournaments.

CHAPTER ELEVEN:
Play the Courses the Tour Professionals Play

"Legendary golfers have cast long and indelible shadows over the game.... Almost every golf course bears the lengthened shadow—the sacred aura—of one particular and special golfer. Over Augusta National and Pinehurst, for example, hang the imposing shadows of Bobby Jones and Sam Snead, respectively.... All golfers walk in the giant shadows of Jones, Snead, and other great champions. Golfers are shadow walkers."
—James Ragonnet, Golf's Three Noble Truths

No one ever learned much by doing the same thing every day, over and over again. To do so would be like learning addition and deciding that any more math would be unnecessary. The same principle applies in golf. As a matter of fact, I am going to raise the bar for learning by suggesting that you arrange to play some professional-level courses while on the back nine of life.

In recent years, many of the tour venues have been opened for access to the average and avid golfer (you and me). What a thrill to play on one of the best courses in the world and then watch, live or on TV, the touring pros play that same course. My challenge to you is above and beyond just playing an unfamiliar course. My challenge is for you to play a spectacular and tour-worthy course occasionally. Here are my reasons.

As an avid golfer, you get to literally walk in the footsteps of giants. You get to tee it up on the same teeing ground as the greats of the game. As a teen golfer, I had a friend whose family belonged to the Atlanta Athletic Club. In the 1960s, the AAC course was East Lake Country Club. By playing there as my friend's guest, I was able to recreate the sights, sounds, and emotions of matches with Bobby Jones, Sam Snead, Arnold Palmer, Gene Sarazen, Walter Hagen, and all the other Hall of Fame golfers who had come before me. They (and I) all had to hit to East Lake's famed island green. I later played three Atlanta Junior Golf Championships and numerous other rounds on this most hallowed venue. Today, you and I can play all the Tournament Players Club (TPC) courses from coast to coast. Many public courses have hosted tour events in the past.

One of the toughest courses I have ever played was the Dinah Shore Tournament Course at Rancho Mirage, California. Lynda and I played it the week prior to the Kraft Nabisco Championship. To play a tour course is the ultimate challenge of your golf skills. In the case of the Dinah Shore, the rough was four to six inches deep, the fairways were as narrow as eyes of a needle, and the greens ran twelve to thirteen on the stimpmeter. I will not reveal my score, but after a day of superb ball striking, I had posted a score that looked more like bowling than golf. It reminded me how good the touring player is. It also reminded me that these conditions are reserved for only the best courses and that playing them ultimately improves my game.

Playing one of the great tour courses always reminds me of the importance of the short game. Most of us do not play courses with tour-speed fast greens with multiple undulations. Nor are most of our greens surrounded by massive bunkers and devilish collection areas that punish anyone unlucky enough to hit the wrong spot on the approach shot. By playing these courses, I am inspired to practice the more creative aspects of the short game, including the use of the putter off the green, the flop shot, and the bump and run. Moreover, playing these courses motivates me to increase my putting drills and seek professional help on how to read greens.

I suggest you play a course with some replica holes. Golden Ocala Golf and Equestrian Club is a mere forty miles from my house and includes replicas from Augusta National (Amen Corner), St. Andrews, Royal Troon, and Baltusrol. I had the pleasure of playing it with Champions Tour player Tom Jenkins. He verified that the replica holes from Augusta were, indeed, authentic.

Summary

- Play a famous course once or more each year.
- Play from the appropriate tees that match your handicap and ability. Playing from the championship tees at TPC Sawgrass may result in physical and mental illness!
- Use the round as a chance to savor the hallowed ground where the giants of the game have walked. Open your senses to the sights, smells, colors, and sounds of the great course.
- Play the round to enjoy the venue and to improve your short game.
- Play a course with replica holes in order to truly feel the shadows of the great players who have won at St. Andrews or Augusta.

CHAPTER TWELVE:
Know the Basic Games of Wagering

"I never rooted against an opponent. But I never rooted for him either."
—Arnold Palmer

"The proper score for a businessman golfer is 90. If it is better than that he is neglecting his business. If it's worse, he is neglecting his golf."
—Rotary Club member, St. Andrews, Scotland

"I play with friends, but we don't play friendly games."
—Ben Hogan

The Basic Nassau
1. Each player puts his ball in a hat. The balls are tossed, and the two balls closest to each other are partners.

2. A coin is tossed between the 2 two-man teams to determine which team goes first in the tee box.

3. The game is called a Nassau. We add a few elements to spice it up. The standard Nassau is three bets in one. We bet a whopping two dollars for the winning team of the front nine, two dollars for the

winner of the back nine, and two dollars for the total round. Your largest win or loss is six dollars per player on a team.

4. The "spices" are the following side bets: one dollar for team birdies, five dollars for team eagles, and one hundred dollars for individual aces (with forty-eight hours to pay the one hundred dollars).

By using full handicaps, the payouts are small or even a wash at the end of the day. Great friendships are made, and each player's focus is sharpened.

There is only one way to poison a fair bet—by not paying your debt or paying late. My friend Jim Mechaney liked to say about golf and poker, "Fast pay makes fast friends."

Here is a rather sad story about failing to pay a debt, and about Jim Mechaney keeping his word. In 2005, I was grouped with Jim and two other club members. We stated the details of the bet on the first tee, as outlined above. On number fifteen I hit the cosmic jackpot and holed out on the 149-yard par 3. Jim Mechaney reached into his back pocket, pulled out a hundred-dollar bill, and gave it to me with a smile and a hearty handshake. One of the other members waited until everyone had hit, got his wallet from his cart, and paid me. The fourth member, a somewhat cantankerous individual, stated, "I *did not* hear the bet," and he refused to pay. Needless to say, his reputation was permanently affected as word of his breech of etiquette spread to other players.

The solution is simple: If you do not want to bet, then do not! The remaining three players have many three-person options or individual games available without you.

Summary

- Know the basic wagers of golf—Nassau, press, carryovers, skins, and other terms.
- Do not be talked into games that you do not understand.
- Be prepared to cover the maximum possible losses.
- Pay off your debts immediately after the round.

CHAPTER THIRTEEN:
Discover and Become Master of Your Golf Temperament

"Golf…is, nevertheless, a game of considerable passion, either of the explosive type, or that which burns inwardly and sears the soul."
—Bobby Jones

"Golf is deceptively simple and endlessly complicated; it satisfies the soul and frustrates the intellect. It is at the same time rewarding and maddening—and it is without a doubt the greatest game mankind has ever invented."
—Arnold Palmer

"Golf is about how well you accept, respond to, and score with your misses much more so than it is a game of your perfect shots."
—Dr. Bob Rotella

After you read this chapter, go to the book's website **www.backninebook.com**, and look for the "Mental Golf Profile" link. This will take you to the website of the *Mental Golf Workshop Profile*, by Bobby Foster. I recommend that you invest in taking the validated DISC assessment that Bobby has adapted from the original DISC instrument. Your results will enhance the reading and learning contained in this chapter. Foster's summary page of the general characteristics of a golfer's temperament is included here for quick reference.

Determining Your DISC Style

Your DISC style might be a Basic Style or a Combination Style. With a basic style, one of the four DISC factors below clearly stands out from the other three factors.

D (Dominance)

- Aggressive   - Strong-willed
- Sense of urgency   - Risk-taker
- Goal-oriented   - Competitive

Players high in the D factor -

Tiger Woods   Phil Mickelson
Greg Norman   Dottie Pepper
Morgan Pressel

S (Steadiness)

- Steady   - Patient
- Relaxed   - Adaptable
- Even-tempered   - Persistent

Players high in the S factor -

Ernie Els   Retief Goosen
Fred Couples   Karrie Webb
Jay Haas

I (Inspiration)

- Enthusiastic   - Creative
- Optimistic   - Spontaneous
- Sociable   - Instinctive

Players high in the I factor -

Brad Faxon   Paula Creamer
Rocco Mediate   Natalie Gulbis
Chi Chi Rodriquez

C (Conscientious)

- Careful   - Logical
- Analytical   - Methodical
- Exacting   - Fact-finder

Players high in the C factor -

Ben Hogan   Se Ri Pak
Jack Nicklaus   Jonathan Byrd
Bernhard Langer

Reprinted with the permission of Bobby Foster, 2012.

The Nature of Temperament

Nobody likes to play with a hothead, sourpuss, or overly serious partner. However, these traits are bad habits developed over the years. I want to discuss a deeper personality-based assessment of how one approaches the game. We will call it "golf temperament." There are four temperaments that a golfer brings to the course and the practice ground. I have created some simple titles or labels for each. Keep in mind that these temperaments are descriptions reserved for the target audience for this book: the senior golfer who has a solid game, a respectable handicap (under 30), and a basic knowledge of the rules of golf.

To borrow liberally from the popular *Personal Profile System©*, each of the four temperaments will be identified by a letter label: D, I, S, or C. Each of the four temperaments (D, I, S, C) will be further explained by the following:

- General behavior and identifying characteristics
- Weaknesses
- Strengths
- Approach to practice

The First Temperament Is the *Director*, or D.

On the course, the D directs the action as in a movie. This player chooses the playing groups, sets the bet or format, and organizes the order of play on the first tee. On the course, the Director will prefer to play fast, ready golf and is generally impatient. The Director is often a good player and suffers in foursomes where one or more players are high (18 plus) handicappers, are beginners, or play at a slow, overly deliberate pace. The D is assertive and/or aggressive both in golf and in life. The D loves a competitive match that plays to his or her strengths.

Weaknesses
- Impatient
- Sometimes rude to other players
- Overbearing
- Hard on other players who lack basic skills, etiquette, knowledge of the rules, or focus

Strengths
- Fast paced
- Skilled player
- Knowledgeable about the basic rules
- Good partner with another skilled player
- Likely to get the game organized and launched

The Second Temperament Is the *Interactive*, or I.

The Interactive golfer is sociable, gregarious, humorous, fun-loving, and fast paced. Like the D, the I likes betting and fast play and has a basic knowledge of the rules. Unlike the D, though, the I lacks the need to control the situation or to play the role of organizer. The goals of the I are to play good golf, have fun, help others have fun, initiate or maintain friendships, and promote harmony within a group or match.

The Interactive is not the person to organize a "golf buddy trip." They rarely play alone and have a speed-dial directory on their cell phones to alert others that they are headed to the course for a few holes or to suggest a tee time for tomorrow. They use the phone as a personal GPS to alert others that they are available for a friendly match or to walk a few holes just before sundown. Their circle of playing partners is deep and wide, and it is important for them to have social time with others before, during, and after any golf event.

Weaknesses
- Can be unfocused and a bit "flaky"
- May have a sense of humor that irritates the other temperaments
- Knowledgeable about the rules, but may suspend them occasionally so as not to offend another player
- May be too talkative

Strengths
- Likely to set upbeat and fun expectations for the round
- Rarely ill-tempered or moody
- Generous and kind

- A sought-after playing partner in informal events (e.g., scrambles, couples events, putting contests, charitable tournaments)

The Third Temperament Is the *Steady*, or S.

The S enjoys order, repetition, team formats, and quiet dignity and harmony. Their ideal day on the course is with their regular foursome, playing the same game EVERY time with the same bets placed EVERY time and playing from the same tees EVERY time on Tuesdays, Thursdays, and Saturdays EVERY week. They are loyal and supportive friends, but lack the exuberance of the Interactive. They are low-key, affable, and respectful of others and the game of golf.

The S is big on tradition, and when not playing the game, he or she enjoys watching the Majors on TV. The opening theme to the Masters brings tears to the S's eyes, and the sound of bagpipes can bring on public sobbing. Their equipment is always clean, and their clubs are arranged in the "right" order in their bag. They can be seriously competitive, but they prefer being part of a team event (Ryder Cup style) than a "play your own score only" event. They are superb diplomats and are adept at settling on-course disputes in a dignified and win-win manner.

Weaknesses
- Adverse to changes in playing partners, playing times, days of play, and any other part of the established routine

- Needs playing partners who are of similar competency and sincerity
- Has some difficulty dealing with conflict and may not respond to arguments or challenges from others

Strengths
- Consummate team player
- Low-key and methodical
- Will help with rules decisions if asked
- Diplomatic and kind
- Honorable and honest
- Great candidate for tournament committees as a "doer" of details

The Fourth Temperament Is the *Cautious*, or C.

The C's are the analytical, precise, serious players. They have saved every scorecard from every course they have ever played, have maintained an official USGA handicap for all their playing years, know the rules of golf, and may be rules officials. They play a focused, serious, loner-style game and concentrate on game improvement, fastidious care of their equipment, and adherence to the rules. They plan their annual playing schedule each year and construct a budget for fees, travel, and equipment changes. Generally, the C is a low-handicap player, conservative in his or her approach to course management, cordial, but not effusive or fiercely competitive. In competition, C's will not hesitate to call a rules infraction on themselves or others. The C is a good teammate, as he or she can be relied upon to play his or her best golf all the time.

Weaknesses
- Overly serious during a round
- Stickler for the rules
- Does not enjoy "fun games" like greenies, sandies, or bingo, bango, bungo; prefers straight-up, by-the-book golf
- May become moody if the game is not going well and is embarrassed by poor performance and failing to meet his or her own goals

Strengths
- A willing scorekeeper, accurate and precise
- Shows up early for a match
- Insists on clarifying the format of the match
- Cordial and polite

Approaches to Game Improvement and Practice (D, I, S, and C)

D's do not enjoy practice. They would rather play their way out of a slump or swing flaw. On rare occasions, they will seek the advice of a professional teacher. This desperate move on their part may be motivated by the prospect of an upcoming tournament or match with an important client. The greatest fear of the D is public humiliation, and they want to have their sharpest game ready for the upcoming event. However, they will only want a "tweaking" of their current swing and will ask the pro to limit the teaching to a few pointers. Following the lesson, the D will hit balls furiously for half an hour, and then resume playing on a regular basis with little or no further practice or follow-up.

The I's use the practice range as a social-networking site. Their practice time is consumed with talking to other players, telling jokes, and catching up on club gossip or personal news. Many times they will cease practice, pull up a chair behind a player, and talk to him or her as the player hits balls. The I is quick to ask for advice from another player as a way to start or continue a conversation.

S's are both amiable and methodical on the practice range. In most cases, they are not practicing to make big changes in their swing, but rather working methodically on becoming more consistent. They will frequently seek out the advice of a professional and are ideal students. They will leave a lesson with a plan of action and will follow it to its conclusion.

The C's will bring technology and analytical processes to the practice range. They have their own video system, a rangefinder, alignment sticks, and a predetermined practice routine. In between practice sessions, the C reads the most recent issues of *Golf Digest* and *Golf Magazine* and watches *The Golf Fix* on the Golf Channel. Since perfection is a common goal of many C's, their practice routine is a scientific application of fundamental principles and golf biomechanics. They tend to practice alone and know when the range will be least populated on any given day. They have identified their playing weaknesses and will spend the majority of their practice session on the measurable improvement of a flaw or weakness. The C's practice sessions are similar to those of the pros.

The Value of Balancing Our Temperament

While each of us has a default temperament, both on the course and on the practice range, we also have all four of the classic temperaments at some level of intensity in our psychological make-up. From situation to situation, we have the ability and choice to utilize our other three temperaments to make our own golf game and the golf experience for our playing partners more enjoyable. The fact is that we cannot change other people. We can only change our own perspectives and enjoy the differences that our playing partners bring to the game—and to life in general.

For instance, the D's can play a casual round with less intensity and offer to help those who respect D skills.

The I's can focus on the competitive nature of a match and be encouraging, not just a source of humor, for the team or group.

The S's can choose to play with new members or different partners, demonstrate the value of team-work, and provide gentle reminders about eti-quette and basic rules.

The C's can volunteer to keep score and share suc-cessful experiences or anecdotes from their newest practice "gizmo." They can choose to appreciate the humor, diplomacy, and focus that the other temperaments bring to the course.

Note: I have used the DISC assessment in my con-sulting practice since 1979. I have a few observa-tions about the idea of temperament or behavioral style.

1. As I mentioned, we all have a "go to" or primary temperament. Our temperament may be so singu-lar that D, I, S, or C may describe us completely. My experience is that we commonly combine our pri-mary temperament with our secondary or backup one. I will use myself as an example. In a casual round, I am a strong I. So I employ lots of humor and encouragement to my group of competitors. The round is basically a walk in a beautiful park.

2. As a competitor in an official event, I am com-bination of I and C. I am friendly, but work to stay focused on my pre-shot routine, clearing my mind for the "Play Box" and concentrating on the short game. I also work very hard to remain calm and

relaxed. My main thought is to keep my tempo at its natural pace. I am approachable and affable, but less so than in a casual match.

3. Stress may affect our temperament and cause us to abandon the player and person that we authentically are. Personally, I play fast and consider a four-hour-and-fifteen-minute round to be acceptable. When play is slow (as in a full-field charity scramble), and we are waiting on every shot for the group ahead to play, I have to fight hard to keep my tempo and focus. The best antidote is to accept the situation and relax. Players tend to get stressed about conditions of play that are beyond their control. Accept, breathe deeply, smile, talk with your teammates about light subjects (no politics, religion, or personal complaints), and stay loose.

Use Your Knowledge of Temperament for Good, Not Evil

You can use information about a competitor's temperament in two ways.

Using Temperament for Good

Honor the competitor's temperament and make slight adjustments to support him or her. I am not asking you to slow down, or to speed up the pace to that of a ferret. It is about little things.

The following suggestions are offered to help you showcase your sportsmanship when playing with competitors:

- If you are playing with D's, acknowledge their good shots and DO NOT comment on their bad shots.

- When playing with I's, smile at their jokes and forgive them if they leave clubs next to the green on every third hole.

- If you are playing with S's, thank them for their advice about rules and compliment their contributions to the team if appropriate.

- If you are playing with C's, notice their preferences and support them. One of my frequent competitors enjoys keeping score and wants to hear each player state his or her score for the hole just played immediately after completing it. The C wants to file an accurate scorecard at the end of the round and wants to verify scores before memory fades as the players advance to the next hole.

Using Temperament for Evil—The Gamesman
I have no patience with these characters and rarely play with them, unless a blind-draw situation forces us to be competitors or partners. The worst

of the breed are the subtlest. In most cases, they ask a question that raises doubt about your game or challenges your temperament. Over time, they become solitary figures with whom no one will play. In some cases, I also know them as clients for my consulting practice. Their gamesmanship may spill over from their business role or even their family history.

A few examples of gamesmanship that come to mind are players who constantly compare your game to theirs and offer relentless, never-ending advice on how to play like they do. Also, direct attacks on your temperament can be withering. Several years ago, I played a round with a member of the country club where my consulting engagement was held. We had identical handicaps, and he was cordial and helpful about the landscape of his home course, until I surged four strokes ahead midway through the back nine. He turned sarcastic and belligerent and mentioned that my tempo and swing were "just too pretty to hold up much longer." He went on to say that many of my shots were a result of lucky bounces, as I did not *really* know the course. My first thought was, "Do I have a lazy swing? Should I swing harder?" My long-time trust in my swing overwhelmed my doubts and my temptation to point out that my "host" must be a "reverse sandbagger," a player who lists a handicap to impress people but cannot achieve it. His behavior is a form of narcissism or, at best, a deep insecurity. The story ends with his abrupt departure from the course. No handshake, no post-round invitation for a drink. When I went into the pro shop to buy a few mementos of a good round on a beautiful course, the head pro came out of his office and apologized for pairing me with that member. Perhaps I was one of many visitor victims of our evil friend?

Summary

- Remember that we all possess a particular golf temperament.
- Recall that if we understand how to use that temperament to play better, it is powerful knowledge.
- Keep in mind that each temperament has strengths and weaknesses. Play to your strengths and get help with your weaknesses.
- Use your knowledge of a competitor's temperament to encourage and support his or her strengths. You will play better as a result.
- Resist using knowledge of a competitor's temperament to employ gamesmanship and psychological trickery. Be your authentic self and strive to elevate the game with proper etiquette and admirable ethics.
- Stick to your own temperament, tempo, and swing when forced to play with a gamesman.

Note: While I wrote this chapter several months before I talked to Bobby Foster and personally took his assessment, our perceptions and conclusions are very similar. I chose to lead you to his official assessment rather than reinvent the wheel and design my own assessment. His golf version of DISC is valid and has been tested and approved by some of the greatest golfers and golf teachers in the world.

CHAPTER FOURTEEN:
Periodically Play in an Official Competition

"Golf is played, for the most part, without the supervision of a referee or umpire. The game relies on the integrity of the individual to show consideration for other players and to abide by the rules. All players should conduct themselves in a disciplined manner, demonstrating courtesy and sportsmanship at all times, irrespective of how competitive they may be. This is the spirit of the game of golf."
—The United States Golf Association, Golf Etiquette 101

"There are two distinct kinds of golf—just plain golf and tournament golf. Golf—the plain variety—is the most delightful of games, an enjoyable, companionable pastime; tournament golf is thrilling, heartbreaking, terribly hard work—a lot of fun when you are young with nothing much on your mind, but fiercely punishing in the end.... The most important part of preparing for a tournament is to condition oneself mentally and physically so that it will be possible to get the most out of what game one possesses."
—Bobby Jones, Bobby Jones on Golf

The author at the Bobby Jones gravesite, Oakland Cemetery, Atlanta

Many people acknowledge Bobby Jones as the greatest golfer the game ever produced. Basically, he felt that there were two forms of golf. One form was casual golf among friends with little or nothing on the line. The objective of casual golf was to enjoy the game and the company of your companions. The other form of golf, according to Jones, was competitive or tournament golf.

Here is my understanding of competitive golf:

1. The USGA rules are strictly followed. No mulligans, no gimmies.

2. The round or tournament is sponsored by an organization or club that has a committee to settle rules disputes. Typically, a PGA professional is on this committee.

3. The round is not complete until the player and one competitor sign each other's scorecards. The score is then verified by the tournament scorer and posted.

This sounds simple and logical, doesn't it? What we know from studies of "casual" versus "competitive" is that our brains work in different ways in each situation. Whether it is a card game like bridge or a chess match or a seemingly harmless game of ping-pong, once it is sanctioned as a tournament game with official rules and judges or referees, our stress level skyrockets. If we rarely play competitively, we tend to defer to one of the three primitive stress responses: fight, flight, or flow. In golf, if the stress is overbearing, we start making mistakes, missing short putts, shanking approach shots, hitting out of order, and failing to record a proper score, resulting in our disqualification from the match or tournament.

I believe that playing periodically in official competition will benefit the senior player, and it will improve the quality of his or her game.

In golf, the "fight" response is observed in a player who loses his or her temper, swings harder than natural, or berates his or her competitors. The fight response is basically a loss of self-control on the player's part.

The "flight" response to stress is to give up, leave the course, and be marked on the scoreboard as NC (no card, no score posted for the round). Another flight response is to withdraw from wagers and state that you are "just playing for fun."

The "flow" response allows us to give up, not care, finish the round, and go home. Flow is stated by a player as, "I am having a bad round, and I do not care." This is not the same kind of flow that some authors have used to describe a state of peak performance, such as, "The winner of the downhill Super G ski race was really in the flow today!"

Deal with the Stress of Competition by Using FOCUS

A fourth alternative to fight, flight, or flow is FOCUS. If you examine the scorecards of the tour winners week after week, you rarely see a round without a bogey or two, or even the occasional dreaded double bogey. However, it is common to see the double bogey followed by a birdie or even eagle. The winner leaves the bogey on the previous hole and plays the next hole as a totally fresh opportunity. When you see players post a series of "train wrecks" that ultimately ruins a round of golf, the player has lost focus. The more competitive events in which you play the more you develop the power of focus, and your scores improve.

Another possible bonus is that by improving your power of focus, you may ward off the onset of age-related memory problems. I realize that I am passing into a sensitive subject, but all the studies I have read indicate that activities that promote repeated focus may force the brain into an active state and may decrease the progression of dementia as we age. When we have to remember the order of cards played in bridge or how many strokes we have taken on a par 5, we are forced to evoke the power of focus.

Sources of Competitive Golf
The most reliable source of competitive golf for seniors is the United States Golf Association (USGA). There is a chapter of the USGA in every state, and most of them sponsor tournaments. Many are flighted to allow players of all levels to compete. Some are multiday, tour-style tournaments, while others are one-day events. Some are individual events, and others feature team formats. Personally, I enjoy playing in the Florida State Golf Association (FSGA) one-day net events. I am able to play in the Super Senior (sixty-five and older) Division with my full handicap. We play beautiful courses like Black Diamond, TPC of Tampa, Innisbrook Copperhead, TPC Sawgrass, Golden Ocala, and other tour venues for a fraction of the usual cost. Officers and

volunteers of the FSGA and USGA run the tournaments like official tour events.

The ultimate source of competitive golf is your individual desire to play the game as it was invented. Play locally with players whom you know play the game straight up, with a small wager on the match to increase your power of focus. Play in your appropriate flight in your club or course championship when possible.

Note: I stated early in this book that I was on a mission to overcome some life-threatening physical setbacks that had devastated my beloved golf game. In the summer and fall of 2011, I won two FSGA one-day net-score tournaments. The final event of my season was at Golden Ocala. Due to the reputation, condition, and private status of the course, the field was at capacity with ninety-seven players. Forty-eight of these were in my age flight. I began the round with back-to-back birdies. At the end of the day, I had carded a gross score of 74; by subtracting my current handicap of 10, my net score was a 64. I won my flight by four strokes and shot the lowest gross (74) for the entire field of ninety-seven players.

Summary

- Play in official competitive events that challenge you to play the game of golf as it was meant to be played.
- Test your responses to stress by playing tournament golf. You can fight, flee, flow, or FOCUS.
- Learn to FOCUS because it is so powerful that it may postpone the inevitable onset and advance of age-related memory loss.

CHAPTER FIFTEEN:
Live a Balanced Senior Life as a Pathway to Better Golf

"There is an Indian proverb or axiom that says that everyone is a house with four rooms, a physical, a mental, an emotional, and a spiritual. Most of us tend to live in one room most of the time but, unless we go into every room every day, even if only to keep it aired, we are not a complete person."
—*Rumi Godden,* A House with Four Rooms

"Philosopher Herb Shepherd describes a healthy, balanced life around four values: perspective (the spiritual), autonomy (the mental), connectedness (the social), and tone (the physical). George Sheehan, the running guru, describes four roles: being a good animal (physical), a good craftsman (mental), a good friend (social), and a saint (spiritual)."
—*Skip Everitt*

"Sharpen the saw basically means expressing all four motivations. It means exercising all four dimensions of our nature, regularly and consistently, in wise and balanced ways."
—*Stephen Covey,* The Seven Habits of Highly Effective People

Our Larger Life

I want to take a break from discussing golf and shift to a discussion about our larger life, the portfolio of life made up of our physical, mental, social, and spiritual dimensions. One of the big mistakes I see retired seniors make is to slip into a life of unhealthy physical habits, reduced emphasis on lifelong learning, limited or "toxic" social activities, and limited spiritual components of a "life well lived."

I am NOT going to discuss your financial portfolio. If this component of your life is not in order by age sixty or so, then I doubt that you are playing much golf. Most likely, you are continuing to work to pay monthly bills and to somehow save enough to truly retire in several years. I do not mean to give finances such a short treatment, but if you are plagued with worry about money, this book is a bit premature for you.

We ALL Know "Roy"

I personally believe that the balanced life enhances one's golf game. As an example of a senior golfer who suffers from a lack of balance, let us follow "Roy" around for a typical day in his life. Roy was a computer-hardware salesman who retired at age fifty-five with a nice pension and an adequate investment portfolio. In the 1960s, Roy served in the military for one four-year tour of duty. Roy was married to Jan, a full-time nurse. They have no children. Roy is an avid golfer with a 16 handicap and a pit bull attitude. Frankly, he has not gotten over possessing the power he once had, both as a soldier and as an account executive.

Playing golf with Roy is generally unpleasant. He is overweight, drinks alcohol excessively, and is argumentative and disagreeable. He is a constant complainer and uses crude and inappropriate humor. He rarely reads books, never attends the local theatrical opportunities that abound in our community, and does not have a church community or any form of spiritual practice. Roy believes that charity is wasted on the weak and unlucky.

When I met Roy seventeen years ago, he was a 10 handicap and at least a tolerable playing companion. As the years passed, his golf game deteriorated, he became cynical, and his health worsened. Three years ago, he moved to a true "senior golf community" because he had alienated all of his playing companions in his current community. I hear that he is unhappy, alone, and physically deteriorating.

The pursuit of an elegant, difficult game like golf should be a happy one.

The Search for Happiness
The research on happiness is clear. From the work of Martin Seligman, M.D., in his book *Flourish*, we learn that happiness is made up of living a life of

creativity, love of learning, integrity, kindness, fairness, humility, gratitude, vitality, spirituality, humor, and love. In his study of the happiest places in the world, *National Geographic* writer Dan Buettner found that happiness was based on meaningful work, lifelong learning, relative equality among citizens, generous public services (transportation, education, healthcare, and cultural experiences), and strong social networks such as family and friends.

Frankly, I believe that life balance puts golf in perspective. A bad day on the golf course does not define your worth as a kind and loving spouse, parent, and grandparent. A three-putt on the last hole can all but be erased from memory with twenty minutes of swimming, biking, or talking with your granddaughter. Admittedly, playing well provides a sense of accomplishment and even sheer joy. My advice? Play hard, practice right, enjoy even a "good walk spoiled," and cherish the memories of one-putts, straight drives, and sand saves. For many of us, golf is a passion. However, like any other sport or hobby, it should not define our existence or keep us from thriving in the other roles of our later lives.

Buettner suggests that we have a small space in our house that is a shrine to our life balance. Mine is in the corner of our home office and contains my three hole-in-one plaques, the scoreboard from my senior club championship victory, artwork from my granddaughter Rachel, and an award plaque from the University of Florida. What, no family photos? Actually, our entire house is decorated with family portraits, vacation photos, and photos of our elders. "Golfer" is a role I serve. The idea of a "portfolio life" in which we carefully choose and define our key roles will ultimately bring great joy to our lives and those around us.

If you are interested in a deeper look at this idea, I recommend two books: *The Portfolio Life*, by David Corbett, and *First Things First*, by Roger and Rebecca Merrill.

Summary

- Commit to living your Back Nine in an intentional and balanced way.
- Remember that balance is achieved by distributing our energy in four life domains: the mental (learning), the physical (health, fitness, and sports), the social (friends and family), and the spiritual (our faith and congregational relationships).
- Keep in mind that happiness is a result of living the balanced life.

CHAPTER SIXTEEN:
Overcome Setbacks and Slumps

"It's not so important what you accomplish in life that matters, but what you overcome that proves who you are."
—Johnny Miller

One of the surest bets you can make on your own golf game is that there will be slumps. In its early stages, a slump is an inexplicable downturn in one or several parts of your game. Many times, a slump begins as a train wreck. The driver with which we could shape shots just last week suddenly becomes an uncontrollable source of worm burners, duck hooks, rainbow slices, pop flies, and housel rockets. There are other golf-specific nicknames for bad shots, but I felt that five were enough to describe the misery of a bad drive. The slump is then fertilized by our attempts at self-correction. We change our swing, play more rounds, hit more practice shots, read more golf instruction books, and (in an act of utter desperation) ask our partners to offer their suggestions.

At this point, I wish I could give you a shortcut to breaking a slump or recovering from an injury or illness. I cannot. Basically, you must go back through Jimmy Roberts's advice, get some help, and be patient. In the two years since that fateful swing that doubled me over with pain and took my breath away, I have diligently followed the path to recovery outlined in this book. My journey back to a respectable golf game has not been without bumps in the road. Despite increasing my fitness and nutrition regimes, the spondylolisthesis returned in early 2010. I was back to hitting 150-yard drives and dreading hitting any shot that required going down and through the ball (90 percent of effective golf shots are in this category). The difference this time was the speed of recovery. Since I knew the symptoms all too well from the episodes of 2008 and 2009, I did not hesitate to ask my internist for a referral to physical therapy. I continued to do daily stretching exercises and spent time on my stationary bike, but I suspended Pilates until the pain began to lessen. Within three months, I was swinging freely and had regained most of my swing speed.

New Equipment, New Attitude, and Better Swing Mechanics

Following this physical recovery, I decided to take radical action: a complete equipment makeover. For ten years, I had played with the same irons, a hodgepodge of drivers and utility clubs, and a garage-filling number of putters. Today, only my old Rossi II putter and Titleist lob wedge remain in my bag. The putter is in imminent danger of being rotated to the dreaded "dark place" (the storage closet) and may not make it to the summer season. My new set of irons, fairway woods, and hybrids are a custom-fitted set of game-improvement clubs. My new shafts are graphite "R" (Regular) stiffness versus my old "S" (Stiff) shafts. My driver is a custom-fitted Ping G5 built by master club fitter Ricky Strain.

Accept Your Real Distances for Each Club

As much a factor as any of the above is identifying and accepting my new, realistic distances for each club. I am reluctantly giving up the notion that I can hit an eight iron 155 yards, or a four-hybrid two hundred yards. One of the mistakes I see my long-time playing partners make is to stick doggedly to old expectations about distance. Their approach shots in particular are chronically ten to twenty yards short of the green. Since they have not worked diligently on their short games, their scrambling percentages are dismal, many times taking three to four shots to finish the hole from thirty yards away. I appreciate Tom Jenkins's advice from the foreword of this book. He reminds us to step back a bit during a slump and concentrate on our scoring game—the chipping and putting.

Recently, I shot a smooth 46 on the front nine of our Saturday men's association tournament. I thought about the words of Jimmy Roberts, Tom Jenkins, and other wise golfers. On the tenth tee, I took a deep, cleansing breath, set my posture in the Pilates "neutral" position, slowed down my pre-shot routine just a bit, and hit my best drive of the day. The ensuing 35 on the back nine brought me back to my goal of "on handicap or better"—a net score of 71.

Slumps will be a part of a golfer's life, but sooner or later they can be overcome with focus, practice, rest, and persistence.

Note: As I write this chapter, my game is finally recovering from the "train wreck" of 2008 to 2010. In March 2011, my brother-in-law invited me back as his member-guest. Remember, we finished dead last in 2010. In 2011 we clawed our way back up to a third-place finish and could have finished higher if a few putts had fallen.

Summary

- Remember that slumps happen. Rarely are they explainable in the moment, and they may grow in size and level of misery very quickly.
- Seek help from teachers and instructional media if a slump becomes a long-term problem.
- Consider evaluating your equipment, swing mechanics, and attitude as you work on a serious slump.
- Stay positive. Playing harder, meaner, faster, or with a gloom-and-doom outlook will only prolong the slump.
- Take a break from competitive golf and work on your game as if you were a novice. Start with the short game and work up to the full swing and long game. Build confidence in one aspect of your golf game at a time.
- Play non-golf games or sports that develop hand-eye coordination, balance, strength, and focus.

Note: Watch the film *Seven Days in Utopia* to see some examples of non-golf games and sports. In the movie, Robert Duvall's character, Johnny Crawford, serves as a mentor to young mini-tour player Luke Chisholm. To help Luke break a terrible slump, Johnny includes fly-fishing, coin-flipping, painting, and piloting a small airplane as ways to refocus the discouraged player. Jimmy Roberts also recommends this technique in his book *Breaking the Slump*.

CHAPTER SEVENTEEN:
Dress and Behave
Like a Competent Player

"The main thing is to dress appropriately. If you are going to play golf, wear golf clothes; if tennis, wear flannels. Do not wear a yachting cap ashore unless you are living on board a yacht."
—*Emily Post,* Etiquette in Society, in Business, in Politics and at Home

In an edition of *Golf Digest* several years ago, golf-fashion guru Marty Hackler wrote a great article on dressing to look your age while staying up to date and stylish. Somewhere between Ricky Fowler and Craig Stadler are a plethora of professional-level outfits for those of us who are in our senior years and who may not possess the flat belly of days gone by.

Generally, the rules are similar to those of tasteful fashion. A light shirt with matching pants or shorts, or dark combinations, has a slimming effect. Vertical and subtle stripes are preferable to horizontal stripes. At the risk of leaving out some acceptable brands, I recommend the newer self-wicking synthetic wear by Nike, Callaway, and Cutter and Buck, and the more conservative styles from Adidas, Taylormade,

Footjoy, Slazenger, Annika, and Bette and Court. I defer to any latest issue of *Golf* or *Golf Digest* for examples. By the way, cotton is OUT, period.

Skip and Lynda Everitt in tournament attire

In terms of shoes, Footjoy continues to lead the way, but several brands have provided us with great choices. Specifically, Adidas, Callaway, Ecco, Puma, and Etonic are good choices. The subject of shoes leads me to go on yet another rant: Shoes are made for walking. Golf was invented as a walking sport. If you are able, WALK. Walking is the number-one best exercise for seniors. Invest in good shoes and, when the course allows, walk. More and more, courses discourage walking by design or necessity, but many of the older, classic courses (like the Atlanta Athletic Club) encourage walking and still expect you to finish a round in four hours and fifteen minutes.

A Simple Technique to Look and Feel Younger

A significant way to look and feel younger is to play FASTER. As I prepare to be a USGA rules official, the biggest problem cited by veteran officials is pace of play. Tournaments are especially vulnerable to slow play because the rules may dictate slow play regarding lost balls, out-of-bounds and rules exceptions, and ensuing decisions. In a casual round, play to the rules as much as possible. The following actions and activities are causes of slow play among senior (and other) golfers:

1. Pre-shot routine (several practice swings, backing off a shot after taking a stance and addressing the ball, excess waggling, re-teeing the ball, and starting up a long-winded story just before you tee it up).

2. Slow movement. Generally moving slowly to and from one's cart or walking extremely slowly.

3. Backtracking. By leaving your cart, bag, or clubs behind as you finish the hole, you must walk

backward away from the next tee, and you will slow up the whole foursome.

4. Slow (glacial) putting. I blame televised professional golf tournaments as one culprit. Here is a pre-putt routine for most of us: Stand or squat behind the hole. You should have looked at the putt from the opposite side as others were putting. Decide on a line. Set your grip. Walk two to three steps and take your stance. Ground your club. Take one more look at your chosen line. Putt. Elapsed time: eleven to fifteen seconds. If your putt is a tap-in, TAP IT IN. Continuous putting saves significant minutes per round.

Be Energetic

Walk with a spring in your step. Use one of the new three-wheel pushcarts made by Sun Mountain or Bag Boy. In lieu of pushing a cart, if your back and spine are in good shape, carry a lightweight bag with only five to seven clubs. The big surprise will be that your score will be as good or even better than if you had carried the legal fourteen clubs!

Summary

- Purchase golf clothing that strikes a balance between the overly youthful and the "old and rumpled" look.
- Buy stylish and comfortable shoes and walk as much as possible.
- Play faster. Check your pace of play, particularly while preparing to putt. Step up the pace of every shot ever so slightly.
- Be an energetic player. Advance your pace of play with a spring in your step, good cart-position management, and good posture.

CHAPTER EIGHTEEN:
The Master Checklist—Reminders for Before, During, and After Each Round

Before Each Round

- Allow fifteen minutes minimum for stretching. Emphasize stretches that work on torso rotation and hamstrings.

- Get to the course forty-five minutes to an hour before your tee time. Hit ten warm-up shots with a short iron, then chip and putt for fifteen minutes, and end with hitting shots that simulate playing the first three holes on the course. End with ten more shots with the same short iron as before to restore tempo.

- Continue to do minor stretching at the first tee. Visit **www.backninebook.com** and watch me demonstrate full stretching routines and "emergency" warm-ups for when stretching or warm-up time is limited. Use a golf cart as a stretching device.

- Concentrate on tempo and balance when it is your turn to tee off. Your goal is to hit the ball in the fairway. Nothing ruins a round of golf quite like a train wreck on the first hole.

During the Round

- Stretch ever third hole. Watch for this with the pros in tournaments on TV. They do it.

- Keep the advice of LPGA professionals Pia Nilsson and Lynn Marriott on your "front screen." In their excellent book, *Play Your Best Golf Now*, they remind us that "there is, as in all areas of life, a time for thought and a time for action—a time to be in the Think Box and a time to be in the Play Box." The Think Box is your pre-shot assessment of distance, lie, outside factors, target and club selection. In the Think Box, you commit to the shot. As you begin your pre-shot routine, you mentally cross the Decision Line and enter the Play Box. Nilsson and Marriott state that "in the Play Box, you must be totally present and through your senses completely engaged with your swing and the shot." Cease continuing to engage in "thought clutter and doubt." The only thought that works in the Play Box is TRUST.

- Between holes, fill in your Improvement Tracker that tracks the five vital statistics from Chapter Two. A pocket-sized printable version of the Improvement Tracker is available at **www.backninebook.com**. My personal experience is that the exercise of keeping the Improvement Tracker up to date helps you stay focused and clears your mind for the next hole.

- As the round progresses, check the status of your golf temperament. Play your own golf temperament and do not be distracted by the personalities of others in your group. If your round starts to deteriorate, consider the following responses for each golf temperament to get back on track:

Director (D): Play a bit more conservatively than usual for a few holes and post some good scores. Pay special attention to grip tension, and take a couple of deep breaths. If a member of your group is driving you crazy through slow play or incompetence, try to refocus on your own game. If a playing partner's swing or behavior bothers you, literally look away or down at your shoes as he or she swings. This may sound a bit odd, but seeing a bad swing over and over again can affect the play of a D, who cannot understand why this person is not a better player.

Interactive (I): Back off cheerleading the foursome. Concentrate on your own game and match the focus and pace of the better players in the group.

Steady (S): Check your level of stress, stretch, and take a few deep breaths. Check your grip pressure and then swing with an emphasis on tempo. Resist the temptation to "steer" the ball, and check your course management. Hit to targets that favor your most reliable clubs. Also, after you determine the distance to a guarded green, choose one club longer and choke up your grip about an inch, then take a full swing.

Cautious (C): Relax and breathe deeply. You have had a few bad holes, but there are plenty left for you to apply a fix. Use your analytical skills to recall ideas from lessons that get your swing back on track.

- Given the risk of sounding cheesy, literally stop and smell the roses. Most likely you are in a beautiful place with friends or respected colleagues. Notice the beauty and wildlife around you, and think about the effort and thoughtfulness that went into getting the course ready for you. Count your blessings and your bogies. You are outside, playing the greatest game ever.

After the Round
- Be gracious and pay any bets as soon as possible. After a reasonable time to socialize, or waiting for tournament results, exit after shaking hands with your group members.

- Immediately practice the areas of your round that troubled you the most, if time allows. Any professional player will tell you that post-round practice is the most valuable time you can invest in game improvement.

- Go over the statistics you wrote down on your Improvement Tracker as soon as possible after the round. Make journal notes on the back of the form about playing conditions, your level of readiness, and things to work on during your next practice session.

- Take a few more minutes and make an entry in your life journal.

Note: My life journal is my copy of the *Seven Days in Utopia* version crafted and stamped for me by artist Allison Lebaron. Go to **www.backninebook.com** and click on the link to her website.

EPILOGUE:
Age Is a Number;
Golf Is a Game for a Lifetime

"Carpe diem—seize the day, boys. Make your life extraordinary."
—John Keating, Robin William's character in the movie Dead Poets Society

Recently I watched an interview with John Mahaffey on The Golf Channel. John was an All-American at the University of Houston (and on the same team with Tom Jenkins) and a successful PGA and Champions Tour winner. John was asked about succeeding in such a difficult sport. He mentioned that there were five factors that enabled him to become a winner. They are the following:

- Focus
- Good fortune
- Execution
- Commitment to finish the round
- Patience

John is now in his sixties and was asked how success was achieved for seniors. His answer was simple but profound: "For the senior golfer, success is based on what works for him or her under pressure."

The Five Critical Factors for Successful Golf as a Senior Player

I believe that John Mahaffey's five factors are critical for the senior golfer who is a serious player. Let us examine them one by one.

First of all, there is FOCUS. I recently had one of my best rounds going in probably six months. Late in the round I began worrying about a personal issue in my family. The worrying started during a conversation with one of my playing partners about grandchildren and their pets. Thirty minutes later, I had gone from one under par to four over par for the round. I had simply lost my focus. Prior to that conversation I had followed the advice of Pia Nillson and Lynn Marriott and had simply thought about the shot I had to make—the part of the golf swing they call the Think Box—and moved into each shot in the Play Box, devoid of worry or distraction.

In later life, focus is an issue in every part of our daily life. Therefore, we must work consciously to keep focus and sharpness in operating mode in everything we do. From golf to travel to the day-to-day work we must do to keep our lives operating, the concept of focus is critical.

Second, John Mahaffey mentioned GOOD FORTUNE as one of the factors for success. He went on to say that good fortune is usually preceded by hard work and a hopeful attitude. We have all had days when good fortune must have stayed in the fortune cookie. Every slightly mis-hit shot ended up in even a worse situation. Thankfully, we also have days on the course when errant shots seem to find a way out of the rough and onto the fairway on the green. Through practice, a focused and relaxed attitude and a hopeful perspective, we will have those days of good fortune.

I believe that Mahaffey listed EXECUTION as a major factor of success because it is the process of repetition. While each shot you take is a new and one-time experience, your commitment to the game, your practice routine, and your attitude will enable you to execute the shot that you have taken literally hundreds of times. When you execute a successful golf shot, you have again moved effortlessly from the Think Box to the Play Box.

The next success factor for seniors, according to John Mahaffey, is a COMMITMENT to a strong finish for every round. Late in the round, we may be experiencing fatigue or distraction. When you feel that sense of fatigue and distraction, "check your vitals" by making sure that your pre-shot routine, your grip pressure, and your alignment are correct. Commit to a swing that emphasizes balance and tempo. Finish the round in balance, with a relaxed tempo and a positive attitude.

Finally, Mahaffey reminds us to be PATIENT. Every shot is, indeed, a new creation for us. The past is the past, and the next shot is the only shot that counts. During a round is not the time to think about the past or to make a radical change in our pre-shot routine or execution of the shot. Also, remember that some days are better than others. Thankfully, there are good days, great shots to come, moments of good luck, and scores that reflect the best in us.

AFTERWORD
Words of Caution and Encouragement

When I wrote the outline of this book in November 2010, my golf game, physical fitness, and mental outlook were at an all-time low. My self-talk was negative and cynical. Most of the time my thoughts were things like, "I will never get my game back to a single-digit handicap, my ribs and back are permanently damaged, and I will be forced to give up the game that I have loved for over fifty years. I wish I could get my old game back." Then I remembered the words of a very wise man, Stephen Covey, author of the best self-help book I have ever read. Much of his wonderful book *The Seven Habits of Highly Effective People* is about how to change the habits and patterns of behavior that have held us back in the past. One of his quotations that has stuck with me since I first read the book in 1989 is "You can't talk your way out of something that you have behaved your way into." My words of caution to you are, "You can't just wish your golf game to return to its former level of fun and satisfaction." Restoring your game to an acceptable level of fun and satisfaction will require practice, focus, and fitness.

The encouraging message I bring to the conclusion of this book is that HOPE combined with a PLAN of improvement will produce a level of play that will be satisfying and fun, and that will last far into your later life.

In his book *Necessary Endings*, Henry Cloud writes, "Hope comes from real, objective reasons that the future is going to be different from the past." He reminds us that change is dependent upon both hope (our own beliefs about the future) and help from others. Cloud warns us that "wishing" simply comes from your desires or feelings and has no real influence or relevance regarding personal improvement.

Two years ago, I wished that I could still hit a drive 260 yards. Today, I HOPE and believe that through proper practice, choosing the right coach, following a healthy fitness and nutrition routine, and constantly reviewing the eighteen chapters of *The Back Nine: How to Play Your Best Golf EVER in Later Life*, I can reclaim many of the skills and competencies of the past, let go of some of the worthless "wishes" of the present, and move into a personal new reality about my future game of golf.

I am well on my way. Today, my handicap has returned to a single digit, I feel great, and I am playing more competitive golf than ever. In the winter, 2012, I attended my three and one half day certification workshop as a USGA rules official—a guarantee of staying in this game for a long time.

Hope and Hard Work

There is no more complicated sport on the planet than golf. Less than 5 percent of all golfers achieve a handicap of 10 or less. Many of us learned to play the game many years ago. This book is for all of us who have lost our game more than once along life's journey. This book is especially for those of us who have faced setbacks and slumps that made us feel like our time as a player of the greatest game was over.

CONCLUSION
Be the Leader of Your
Own Life and Inspire Others

In my twenty-six years of serving as a consultant and personal coach for dozens of executives and business owners, I was continuously challenged to define and describe "leadership" for my clients and their employees. While hundreds of books have been written about leadership, I have come to a simple conclusion about how people act when they are true leaders. A leader is anyone who has lived a life literally filled with successes AND failures. The difference between leaders and anyone else is defined by how they responded to the failures. A leader—with the help of trusted advisors—figures out the reason for a failure, acts with courage to fix the problem, and is joyful with the results and thankful for all sources of support, information, counsel, and trust.

Restoring our broken game of golf is an act of personal leadership. The willingness and discipline to do the hard work of restoration of our game, and our living of a significant "portfolio life," are the works of leaders. The intention of this book is to provide a blueprint for restoring your game, no matter what your age may be. At this time in life, many of us are "chasing daylight" as we enter our later life. This is no time to give up. This is a time to play the game of golf as well as possible and, in the time that remains, to soak in the beauty of our favorite golf course and the companionship of our partners and competitors.

For many of us, golf has been an important part of a life of meaning and significance. While it is only one "folder" of our life's portfolio, golf is a treasure trove of memories that has shaped our feelings of success, friendship, and happiness.

One way or another, my friend, find a way to stay in the game.

Dr. Skip Everitt
2012

APPENDIX
Additional Helpful Advice

As I started to wind down my writing of this book, I decided to test the ideas contained in the eighteen chapters by discussing them with a few more great players and teachers.

My question to all the interviewees was the same: What advice can you give senior golfers to help them improve and maintain their game?

The first interview was with John Darr, a retired insurance executive in Gainesville, Florida. He is a ten-time winner of the Senior Championship at Haile Plantation Golf and Country Club. While a player and student at the University of Florida, he was a starting player for the 1968 NCAA National Championship team. John coached the University of Florida men's team from 1979 to 1980. He is generous with his advice and teaching, and I feel fortunate to have him as a friend, coach, and competitor.

John's advice for senior golfers:

"It's all about the short game—specifically those shots from less than fifty yards to the flagstick. Find a good short-game practice area. Few courses have them, so you may have to search your area a bit to find one. If one is not available, practice on the course when possible.

"Make up games to force yourself to practice difficult shots.

"Don't be afraid to ask low-handicap golfers to play a round with you. They won't be playing against you. They play against the course. Watch and learn from their games.

"The thing that changed the most for me when I became 'senior' was a move from a fiercely competitive mindset to one of a sense of arrival. I feel much calmer than before."

Details about Vitamin Supplements

The following amounts are from Web MD and represent RDA (recommended dietary allowance). This is not the amount of supplement that you should take, but the total amount, which includes a healthy diet plus supplements.

- B Complex: 1,800 mg (men); 425 mg (women)
- Folic acid: 1,000 mcg
- Calcium: 1,200 mg
- Vitamin A: 2,500 IU

- Vitamin B3: 15 mg
- Vitamin B6:1.5 mg
- Vitamin C: 90 mg (men); 75 mg (women)
- Vitamin D: 15 mg
- Vitamin E: 22.4 IU

The Website and Blog

Additional interviews and links to helpful websites will be posted periodically on www.**backninebook. com**. Visit the website to access videos about practice, fitness and focus. Join the blog and exchange information, opinions, and ideas for maintaining your golf game as you age. Our first edition of the website will feature PGA professional John Reger in a podcast about doing business on the golf course. Also, I will demonstrate how to warm up for a round in just five minutes before tee time. In addition, you will find over a dozen links to additional resources and a blog space.

Acknowledgments

The Back Nine: How to Play Your Best Golf EVER in Later Life was originally launched as my personal journal to describe how I overcame two life-changing physical setbacks to restore my golf game. It grew into a book outline and a sharpened awareness of how many people had helped me to regain my golf game, my dignity, and my resolve to recover. Therefore, these acknowledgements are a bit lengthier than those for the usual nonfiction book. At the risk of leaving someone out, I present the following heartfelt thanks to those who healed me, befriended me, and supported me along this journey of golf and life.

To the M3, "The Mighty Men of MidLife." This group formed over ten years ago as a result of a practice-range conversation with two of my golf buddies. We have met periodically to share a meal, discuss our troubles and our triumphs, and to help each other. The following men are the current members of M3:

Steve Aasheim
Don Balloon
Larry Danek
Bill Evans
Chuck Dolsak
John Gaston

Dale Green
Dick Mahaffey
Wayne McDaniel
Dave Michael
Dick Rosmarin
Chuck Soponis
Richard Wisby

To men who profoundly shaped my life:
Gene Everitt, my dad and the person who thought that a man's education was incomplete without learning to play golf.
Hardy McCalman, my father-in-law with whom I shared many rounds of golf including his last.
Ishma Davis, golfer and gentleman. My first teacher.
James "Chick" Yates, head professional at Candler Golf Course.

To the volunteer members of the Twilight Round Golf Tournament, a charity event cofounded by Cindy Flowers, my wife, Lynda and me in 2004 to honor the memory of Hardy McCalman and to raise funds for our local Alzheimer's Association:
Carol Aasheim
Jill Evans
John Gaston
Amy Kinsey
Marsha Dolsak
Gayle Green
Theresa Williams
Blake Fletcher

Kathi Bellucci
Kathleen Bogolea
Cindy Flowers
Richard Mitchell
Lynda Everitt
Bill Ebersole
Michael Edge
Ginger Leblanc
Brian Early

Within this committee, I extend special thanks to Dr. Bobby Slaton and Wenda Lewis, two tireless, generous, and caring volunteer leaders who refused to settle for anything short of success.

To all my mentors and companions who are volunteer rules officials for the Florida State Golf Association, and to the management and staff of the FSGA home office.

To the professional staff, past and present, of Haile Plantation Golf and Country Club in Gainesville, Florida. A special thanks to those club professionals who took time to play rounds with us members:
Bob Sommers
Tony Wise
Kyle Caudill
Matt Porter

To General Manager Jeremy Little.

To Lydia and Jesse Teasley, masters of warmth and welcoming.

To Joe Holden, our superintendent and a wizard of all things that make our course a fun and challenging venue.

To Sue Mickley, the diva of dining in our grill room at Haile Plantation. Her wit and patience are legendary.

A special thanks to Tommi Ylijoki for his assistance with the on-course lesson described in the book and for his consistent diplomacy as our first assistant professional.

To the Tuesday/Thursday "show up and play" group. Special thanks to Larry Collison and Dick Mahaffey for attempting to manage this group. All of you are good guys and worthy competitors, and indeed, someone will "show up" each and every Tuesday and Thursday morning.

To family who cheered me on to complete the book:

To Simon Patfield, son-in law, for his technical knowledge, patience and willingness to help prepare the manuscript for submission and his design and management of the website.

Robin Patfield, daughter, kind and dear soul, and go-to "listener in chief" for me and others.

David Everitt, son, legal counsel, and lifelong "best bubba."

Christine Everitt, my mother who encouraged me to become a gentleman and who took me to see Hopalong Cassidy in person.

Dot Powell, aunt, second mom, and example of the power of curiosity and positive outlook.

Merryl McCalman, mother-in-law, consummate fan of golf and many other sports, and the epitome of graciousness and gentility.

Mary Covington and Jerry Woods, great travel companions and caring in-laws.

Rachel Emily Patfield, granddaughter, who is in love with each day and thinks I'm funny.

The author and his granddaughter, Rachel Patfield

To Jim Wagner, wise counsel, friend and my first playing partner at Haile Plantation Golf course.

To Barbara Rienzo, a friend who frequently shares our love of the total golf experience—the game, the fellowship, the food and the wine.

To friends and supporters above and beyond the game of golf:

Larry and Sandy Reimer, Mary Anne Wagner, John and Fonda Eyler, Jim and Denis Newman, Brian and Vikki Handley, Michael and Sandi Chance, Jim and Karen Archer, Paul and Reisa George, Fred and Trisha Gregory, and so many other friends who shared their love and fellowship along the way.

Valerie Owens, healer and friend.

Jim Brantley, fixer of all things household and mechanical, and trusted advisor.

To friends who, in different ways, made the book come alive:

Allison Lebaron, artist and designer of the *Seven Days in Utopia* journal.

Greg Whitford, Tom Rothrock, and Paul Hasse, who invited me to join their traveling foursome for FSGA one-day events.

Chris Reimer, friend and PGA staff member, who gets to go to all the cool places and schmoozes with the players—and gets paid for doing these gigs!

To characters, raconteurs, and local celebrities:

Howard Freeman, who teaches all of us the value of charity and the love of competition.

Carl Miller, Burt Hughes, Jack Wicks, Oka Okabe, Lorenzo Lleras, Carl Carlson, Ken Grazioso, Paul and Paul (Ferraro and Gagnon), John Harpe, Larry and Leon Schneider, Bob Roundtree, Bob Fleetwood, Mike Allen, Rusty Dougherty, J.R. Anchors, Dave Cox, Jeff Render, Ron Cordasco, Mark Spiwak, Mark Resler, Rene Brignoni, John Darr Jr., Cleve Cooper, Doug Lanier, and many others who just make life interesting.

In Memoriam:
Charlie Stuart
Jim Mechaney

14702530R00094

Made in the USA
Charleston, SC
26 September 2012

We all say retirement will improve our golf game. Yet when that da
comes, we find both our game and our body in decline. This book is
guide to shaping up your life and your game later in life. This guide
based on the author's personal experience facing setbacks in his golf gam
during his retirement years. A golfer for over fifty years, he found himse
building the best game of his life at age sixty-three. Yet at his golfin
pinnacle, Dr. Skip Everitt was diagnosed with cancer and experience
a series of injuries that dealt him a setback. So he reinvented both h
life and game. He shares his wisdom through eighteen essential lesson
imparted over the course of his book. His goal is to share his experienc
with others who hope to continue their "back nine" in good health, hig
spirits, and top form. This book includes a Foreword by Tom Jenkin
eight time winner on the regular PGA and Champions Tour.

Everitt is a leadership consultant, writer, and avid golfer. For ove
twenty-five years, he has trained thousands of leaders in developin
teamwork and communications. His love affair with golf began in hig
school, where he led his team to a first place finish in the 1963 Atlant
High School Championship. In 2008, he auditioned for the Wanderin
Golfer series on the Fine Living Network and finished among the to
twenty-five applicants from a total of over 1,500 entries. Everitt and h
wife Lynda live in Gainesville, Florida.

ISBN 978-1456372170

9 781456 372170